THE FIRST-TIME MANAGER'S GUIDE TO

PERFORMANCE APPRAISALS

Other Books by Diane Arthur

Recruiting, Interviewing, Selecting & Orienting New Employees, Fourth Edition (New York: AMACOM, 2006)

The Employee Recruitment and Retention Handbook (New York: AMACOM, 2001)

Recruiting, Interviewing, Selecting & Orienting New Employees, Third Edition (New York: AMACOM, 1998; also published in the People's Republic of China in 2000)

The Complete Human Resources Writing Guide (New York: AMACOM, 1997)

Managing Human Resources in Small & Mid-Sized Companies, Second Edition (New York: AMACOM, 1995)

Workplace Testing: An Employer's Guide to Policies and Practices (New York: AMACOM, 1994)

Recruiting, Interviewing, Selecting & Orienting New Employees, Second Edition (New York: AMACOM, 1991)

Managing Human Resources in Small & Mid-Sized Companies (New York: AMACOM, 1987)

Recruiting, Interviewing, Selecting & Orienting New Employees (New York: AMACOM, 1986; also published in Colombia in 1987)

Also by Diane Arthur

Performance Appraisals: Strategies for Success (American Management Association Self-Study Division, 2007)

Fundamentals of Human Resources Management, Fourth Edition (American Management Association Self-Study Division, 2004)

Successful Interviewing: Techniques for Hiring, Coaching, and Performance Meetings (American Management Association Self-Study Division, 2000)

Success Through Assertiveness (American Management Association Self-Study Division, 1980)

THE FIRST-TIME MANAGER'S GUIDE TO

PERFORMANCE APPRAISALS

Diane Arthur

AMACOM

American Management Association

New York • Atlanta • Brussels • Chicago • Mexico City • San Francisco
Shanghai • Tokyo • Toronto • Washington, D.C.

This publication is designed to provide accurate and authoritative information in regard to the subject matter covered. It is sold with the understanding that the publisher is not engaged in rendering legal, accounting, or other professional service. If legal advice or other expert assistance is required, the services of a competent professional person should be sought.

Library of Congress Cataloging-in-Publication Data

Arthur, Diane.
      The first-time manager's guide to performance appraisals / Diane Arthur.
          p.   cm.
      Includes index.
      ISBN-13: 978–0-8144–7440–2 (pbk.)
      ISBN-10: 0–8144–7440–3 (pbk.)
      1. Employees—Rating of—Handbooks, manuals, etc.   I. Title.
      HF5549.5.R3A77   2008
      658.3'125—dc22

                                                          2007011452

Printing number

10   9   8   7   6   5   4   3   2   1

Contents

PART III: THE POWER OF THE PEN

PART IV: THE FACE-TO-FACE MEETING

PART V: WHAT TO LOOK OUT FOR

PART VI: EVALUATING VARIOUS TYPES OF EMPLOYEES

Dedication

To My Own Top Performers
Warren, Valerie, and Victoria

Preface

Consider this scenario: You have just been promoted to manager of a department in which you've worked for the past four years, placing you in charge of your former coworkers. You have a keen understanding of how the department functions, along with first-hand knowledge of the challenges associated with each job, but you've never before been a manager.

By way of preparation for your new responsibilities, you've attended workshops and shadowed your predecessor for several weeks, gaining knowledge of key managerial skills such as delegation, decision-making, and time management. With all that you're learning, you feel confident that you'll succeed in your new role.

There is, however, one area that remains somewhat of a mystery: the performance appraisal; that is, evaluating the work of your employees. While you've been on the receiving end of performance appraisals, you never gave much thought to how your manager pulled it all together. Now that it's part of your job, you've got lots of questions: What are you supposed to base the ratings on? How do you complete the form? How do you handle marginal performers, especially when they're your friends? Exactly what is it you're supposed to talk about in the appraisal meeting? What are some of the performance appraisal pitfalls you should avoid?

That's where *The First-Time Manager's Guide to Performance Appraisals* comes in. This handy guide provides straightforward and useful information that will enable anyone to conduct performance appraisals with confidence and skill. You'll learn how to review employees' past performance; assess how successful they've been in meeting previously set performance objectives; help them set new, achievable work performance objectives; and assist them in their pursuit of career development plans.

Each chapter succinctly targets a specific aspect of performance appraisals, supported by practical scenarios, examples and tips, all geared to help you prepare for and conduct maximally effective performance appraisals. In Appendix A, you'll find a summary of 70 tips that will help reinforce what you've learned and serve as a quick refresher when you need it.

Whether you're a newly hired or promoted manager, or an experienced manager seeking an easy-to-follow format regarding performance-appraisal basics, you'll feel more self-assured and capable at the conclusion of *The First-Time Manager's Guide to Performance Appraisals*.

D.A.

·1·

Performance Appraisals: An Overview

The subject of performance appraisals, also referred to as "performance reviews" and "assessments," initially strikes many first-time managers as being complex and difficult. There are images of intricate forms, close scrutiny by Human Resources (HR), legal pitfalls, awkward face-to-face meetings, less-than-favorable reactions by marginal performers, and disputes over recommended salary increases.

In truth, the performance-appraisal process need not be overwhelming or problematic. In fact, it's quite straightforward. The process begins by identifying objectives, recognizing the benefits for all concerned, and identifying key criteria.

Objectives

Think back to the last time your work was formally reviewed. Did your manager make clear the overall purpose of the performance evaluation? Did you appreciate how the process benefited you, your manager, and the organization as a whole? Did you fully understand the key aspects of an effective performance appraisal system? Don't worry if you answered "no" to one or more of these questions. All three are rarely answered affirmatively due, in part, to the fact that many managers fail to have a clear understanding of what performance reviews are intended to accomplish.

Primary Objective of a Performance Appraisal

The primary objective of a performance appraisal is to ensure the maximum utilization of every employee's skills, knowledge, and interests. At first glance, this deceptively simple statement appears to be completely employee-directed. In truth, organizations that focus on the full use of each individual's abilities and areas of interest have a more motivated workforce; this, in turn, positively affects productivity, thereby increasing the company's competitive edge. In the end, everyone benefits. Let's examine this assertion more closely by way of two scenarios.

Scenario Number One: Lorie

Meet Lorie, hired two years ago to work as a computer analyst for a large bank. Employed right out of college, she was selected for the high grades she had achieved in computer science classes, as well as her experience working part-time performing data entry at the local branch of a bank near her school. During her employment interview, Lorie was asked about her knowledge of, and skills working with, computers. She elaborated on the fact that she had always being adept at working with computers. At no time did the interviewer ask Lorie whether she actually enjoyed computer work; nor did he ask her whether her short- and long-term goals involved computers.

Lorie was pleased to receive a job offer so close to graduation, and she gladly accepted. After several months, however, she began to reflect on the advertising classes she'd taken in college, and how much she'd enjoyed them. She wondered whether she'd made a mistake accepting a job working with computers simply because she was good at it.

During her first formal performance assessment, which resulted in a very high rating, she mentioned her interest in advertising. Her boss was chagrined, commenting that she should stick to what she knows and is good at, adding that she could look forward to a bright future with the bank.

Following that meeting, Lorie found herself focusing increasingly on her interest in advertising. Concurrently, her motivation to perform her job duties decreased, as did her performance level. She began to make mistakes—costly mistakes for the bank. Lorie was coached and counseled, but at no time was she asked what she thought was wrong. Finally, just before her next official performance review, Lorie tendered her resignation. During the exit interview with HR she explained that she had accepted an entry-level job at an advertising agency, where she would be able to work at what she really enjoyed.

Scenario Number Two: Vincent

When Vincent began searching for a job in HR, he was in the midst of a well-thought-out career change. He'd been teaching middle-school math for four years but always had an avid interest in the field of human resources. As a result, he returned to school, where he earned a degree in HR. He also interned in the HR department of a resort for two summers. He presented himself to prospective employers as having limited skills and knowledge, but a keen interest in HR.

During an interview for an HR assistant's position at a retail company, Vincent was asked many questions about his interest in HR, as well as the knowledge he'd acquired in school and the experience he'd obtained through his internship. It was evident that Vincent's interest in HR overshadowed his skills and knowledge, but the interviewer felt that the former would make Vincent an asset to the organization. The interviewer's assessment proved to be accurate: Vincent thrived in his position and was ultimately promoted to HR director. His colleagues and employees were motivated by his enthusiasm and energy and felt compelled to work harder. Three years after Vincent was hired, the company was showcased in a trade publication as having an "ideal HR department."

> **• TIP #1 •**
>
> The primary objective of a performance appraisal is to ensure the maximum utilization of every employee's skills, knowledge, and interests.

Secondary Performance-Appraisal Objectives

Performance-appraisal objectives extend beyond the primary focus cited above. They also serve to enhance employer-employee relations. This is accomplished by strengthening the overall working relationship between managers and employees; developing a mutual understanding between managers and employees about performance expectations, goals, and measured criteria; encouraging employees to express themselves openly concerning performance-related issues; encouraging managers to examine their own strengths and areas requiring improvement; and helping managers to coach and counsel their employees as needed.

Performance appraisals also permit HR to perform key tasks more effectively by providing supportive data for decisions concerning salary increases, promotions, and disciplinary action; allowing for more productive uses of an organization's human resources; and yielding information about existing skill levels to support ways to expand beyond the existing talent pool.

In addition, by providing feedback on past performance, evaluating an employee's potential, and supporting developmental opportunities, managers can motivate employees to establish and achieve personal goals that are compatible with organizational goals.

> **• TIP #2 •**
>
> Secondary performance-appraisal objectives include enhancing employer-employee relations; permitting HR to perform key tasks more effectively; and motivating employees to pursue goals that are compatible with organizational goals.

Benefits and Uses

It's not uncommon for both managers and employees to believe that performance assessments should be used to justify salary increases. Actually, many HR experts urge separating the timing of appraisals from when salary reviews are conducted by as much as three months. This way, employees won't think in terms of how their rating translates into dollars; they'll be able, instead, to focus on the specific observations of their appraiser.

So, if performance appraisals shouldn't be used in conjunction with raises, how should they be used?

Benefits and Uses for Managers

Let's start with how performance appraisals benefit you, the manager. First, you will be able to make the best use of your employees' abilities by becoming more aware of each person's strengths and areas requiring improvement. Second, you can isolate atypical employee behavior and performance; that is, you can identify outstanding performers and provide them with additional incentives and more challenging work assignments. You can also spot marginal performers and give them greater guidance and direction. Third, performance appraisals help you become introspective and determine whether you are doing your job as a manager: Ask yourself: *Am I available for questions? Am I clear in my expectations?* The answers to these and other questions will improve overall employer-employee relations. Finally, once employee skill levels are properly identified and you've determined whether you're functioning effectively as a manager, you can focus more fully on developing your own career goals.

Benefits and Uses for Employees

During the review process, managers typically clarify areas of responsibilities. This benefits employees by ensuring a mutual understanding of the scope and nature of their job, negating the likelihood of hearing them say, "I didn't know I was expected to do that!" Employees also learn how well they have been performing in relation to their areas of responsibility. This can lead to a discussion of helpful training opportunities, as well as a dialogue about future goals and career development. The performance-appraisal process additionally affords employees a chance to express openly their views and concerns about anything work-related.

Benefits and Uses for the Organization

Performance-appraisal systems can help protect organizations against discrimination allegations by providing an element of consistency; that is, ensuring that all similarly classified employees are evaluated based on the same criteria. In addition, performance appraisals reveal employee aspirations and career-development plans, thereby allowing organizations to determine whether there is sufficient alignment between their strategic goals and employee goals. Furthermore, data are furnished to help establish equitable and competitive salary-administration programs. Future training and development needs are also identified.

• TIP #3 •

The most effective performance-appraisal programs are those that are beneficial to managers, employees, and the organization as a whole.

Responsibilities

HR practitioners have the greatest scope of responsibility when it comes to performance appraisals. They're expected to apply employment laws; identify the most productive method of appraisal; design evaluation forms that best facilitate the face-to-face meetings between you and your employees; review the content of completed appraisals for consistency between ratings, supporting statements, and any recommendations you've made; and ensure that the performance-review process achieves its primary objective: that is, the maximum utilization of every employee's skills, knowledge, and interests.

As a manager, you're responsible for understanding how employment laws pertain to the performance-appraisal process, and for preparing for and conducting the face-to-face meeting. In addition, you're expected to provide ongoing assistance, support, praise, and constructive criticism (see Chapter 2, "Managers as Coaches") as well as to work with employees on specific work-related issues, as needed (see Chapter 3, "Managers as Counselors").

Employees should also play an active role in the performance-appraisal process. Specifically, they may complete self-appraisals to compare with your evaluation of their work performance; ask questions and express views about their evaluations; and seek job-enhancement and career-growth opportunities.

> **• TIP #4 •**
>
> While HR has the greatest scope of responsibility when it comes to performance appraisals, managers and employees should also actively participate in the process.

Criteria

While, as a first-time manager, you're unlikely to have much say in how your organization's performance-appraisal system is designed, it's helpful for you to understand the following criteria for an effective system. It should be:

Job-Related

A performance program should be founded on criteria that are directly related to the primary duties and responsibilities of a particular job. The criteria should be specific, observable, and measurable; for example, the criteria for a sales representative might include ". . . generating an additional $x,xxx in revenue each month."

The nature and level of responsibility for each position

should determine the amount of weight assigned to each factor measured.

Reliable and Valid

To be reliable, a performance-appraisal system should yield consistent data regardless of who does the appraising or when they do it. For the system to be valid, there must be a direct correlation between the factors being measured and the critical elements of a particular job. Elements critical to one job might not be at all relevant in another job; for example, requiring experience with conflict-resolution would be valid for a customer service representative; it's unlikely to be valid for an administrative assistant.

Standardized

An appraisal program should be standardized in its design and consistent in its administration. This does not mean that you cannot have more than one set of standards: indeed, many organizations have one set of evaluative categories for exempt employees and another for nonexempt employees (the Fair Labor Standards Act defines the term *exempt* as literally meaning "exempt from overtime compensation"; the term *nonexempt* conversely means "not exempt from overtime compensation." The Department of Labor provides a series of requirements that must be met before classifying someone as exempt.)

All managers and HR practitioners using the appraisal system should be given written guidelines accompanied by training in its implementation. Organizations should also develop effective techniques for monitoring the degree of consistency in implementation.

Practical and Workable

To be effective, a performance-appraisal system should be practical, workable, and viewed by managers as a helpful tool. In particular, it should not be so complex or time-consuming to administer that you view it as a burden. This can easily occur when instructions for completion are difficult to interpret, forms are excessive in length, multiple approval steps are required, or the system requires a forced distribution of results.

Acceptable

A performance program should be deemed acceptable by appraisers, the appraised, senior management, and HR; in other words, everyone in the organization. Ideally, representatives from each of these groups should have some role in developing the system; for example, HR may prepare the framework of the system; managers could contribute categories they feel are important; employees might help develop criteria for measuring their own performance; and senior management would show its support of the program via a written message to everyone in the organization.

Managerial Style

Managerial style should be conducive to employee growth. In order to create the right climate for a successful performance-assessment system, you should strive to be encouraging and supportive of your employees' efforts. You should also display confidence in your employees' ability to progress.

Periodically ask yourself questions to determine how well your style relates to performance management; for example, (1) Do I know how my employees view me? (2) Do I have sufficient confidence in my own skills to encourage the growth and development of others? (3) Do I show interest in my employees and exhibit encouragement for greater accomplishment?

If you can answer these questions affirmatively, then be confident that your managerial style is likely to encourage employee growth.

Suggestions for Improved Performance

Managers often shy away from offering suggestions for improved performance. After all, it can be uncomfortable to tell employees that their work is anything less than outstanding, even when their performance is really subpar. Yet, an important element of performance appraisals is offering suggestions for improved performance so employees can strive to use their skills, knowledge, and interests as much as possible.

The key to success is for employees to be receptive to their manager's suggestions. This requires a solid rapport between you and your employees, coupled with mutual respect. If these elements are lacking, employees are unlikely to be responsive to even the most well-intentioned suggestions for performance improvement.

• TIP #5 •

In order for a performance-appraisal system to function effectively, it must be: job-related; reliable and valid; standardized; practical and workable; acceptable to everyone in the organization; reflective of a managerial style that is conducive to employee growth; and predicated on a managerial willingness to offer suggestions for improved performance.

2

Managers as Coaches

Coaching is the day-to-day interaction between you and your employees, whereby you may provide assistance, support, praise, and constructive criticism. It is especially effective when provided on an informal, ongoing basis. Coaching lets employees know what is expected of them and tells them how they're doing. It can help develop needed skills and often heads off potential problems. It is as important for top and average performers as for those needing to focus on improved performance.

Managerial coaching is crucial for making the best use of employees' potential and for keeping them motivated at their jobs. It also contributes toward improving the organization's overall productivity.

> ### • TIP #6 •
> Coaching is the day-to-day interaction between you and your employees. Its purpose is to provide regular assistance, support, praise, and constructive criticism.

Coaching Characteristics

To be an effective coach, you should strive to demonstrate the following characteristics:

Approachability

Whether they need help or want to talk about an idea they have concerning how to proceed with a task, you need your employees to view you as responsive and accessible. Employees should feel that you are available for coaching, at any time and for any reason. Here are some sample statements made by an approachable manager:

- "I know the Johnson report is taking more time than you'd originally anticipated. I just want you to know that I'm available if you want to use me as a sounding board to go over what remains to be done."
- "The idea you submitted to HR about increased production was really innovative. If you'd like to discuss it in greater depth, I'm all ears."

Consistency

To earn the trust and respect of your employees, strive to apply organizational policies, procedures, and rules as even-handedly as possible. Conversely, avoid showing favoritism, bending the rules, or looking the other way, even when it doesn't seem as if any harm will come of it, or if it's unlikely that anyone will find out.

Here's an example: One of your best workers asks for extra time off to take care of "something really important." He's already used up all of his paid leave but wants one additional day off, with pay. You are tempted to grant his request because of his outstanding employment history but realize that doing so could negatively impact the relationship you have with the rest of your staff should they find out you bent the rules or if one of them comes to you with a similar request and you say no because he or she does not have the same stellar performance record. The best thing to do is to say, "I wish I could grant your request, but I'm sure you'll agree that wouldn't be fair to your colleagues. It's important that I remain consistent in my dealings with all of you. I can give you the day off, but, according to policy, it will have to be unpaid."

Dependability

Nothing shakes an employee's confidence more than feeling uncertain about whether he can count on you when needed. Managers who demonstrate that they are reliable are more likely to have maximally effective employer-employee relations.

Consider this as an example of dependability: A recently promoted worker is struggling with her new set of responsibilities. Afraid of looking foolish, she pretends to know how to perform certain tasks. Aware of what's going on, you casually approach her and say, "When I first had your job, I had a million questions. Fortunately, I could always count on my manager to either answer them or steer me in the right direction. I hope you'll consider me to be as reliable a resource."

Empathy

Managers frequently find themselves in the position of listening to employees' work-related and personal problems. When this happens, you must strive to remain impartial, thereby maintaining an emotional distance so you can best help the employee achieve resolution. The key is to be empathetic, not sympathetic.

Here's an example of a *sympathetic* response: "I know exactly what you're going through. When my dad was in the hospital, I couldn't get to work on time either, visiting hours being what they are. I completely relate to how hard this is for you."

Here's the *empathetic* version of that same statement: "I appreciate the fact that it's difficult for you to get to work on time with your dad in the hospital. Perhaps there's a way we can utilize the company's flextime option so you can visit your dad and still come in on time."

Honesty

You should try to be straightforward and forthright without being harsh or disrespectful. This is best accomplished by adhering to the facts in all matters calling for both praise and criticism. For example, "Mike, despite the fact that you fell short of your overall goal of three new clients for the month, you exhibited tremendous effort." Contrast that statement with: "Mike, you still don't seem to be able to reach your overall goal of bringing in new clients even though the other sales reps can."

Knowledge

Smart managers are as clear about what they do not know as they are about what they do know. Smarter still are those who view themselves as lifelong learners. Consider this scenario: Jack approaches his manager, Blair, for help with the project he's working on. Blair is stymied, not having a clue as to how Jack should proceed. She can either give a vague, generalized response in order to "save face," or say, "Jack, I'm afraid I don't know the answer. I do, however, know where you can go for help."

Respect

You cannot demand respect from your employees if you do not offer it. This includes having regard for employees' views, approaches to tasks, requests, and needs. Saying, "I'd like your input regarding how to best go about achieving results" is respectful and much more effective than saying, "Here's the problem, and this is how we're going to solve it."

• TIP #7 •

To be an effective coach, you should strive to be approachable, consistent, dependable, empathetic, honest, knowledgeable, and respectful.

Spontaneous Coaching

Spontaneous coaching requires you to be attentive and attuned to each employee's individual work habits, routines, and current assignments. This principle pertains to both positive and negative performance.

Positive Spontaneous Coaching

Stopping by a worker's desk to say, "Nice job on that monthly report; the summary you wrote clearly explained the sea of numbers preceding it!" is an example of positive spontaneous coaching. Note that the first part of this comment lacks reference to anything specific; left to stand on its own, the generic statement "Nice job on that monthly report" could be perceived as hollow and insincere. Adding details to the observation, however, sends both a clear and sincere message to the employee; that is, you read the report and specifically noted the positive impact of the summary. This example of spontaneous coaching takes less than 10 seconds to accomplish; yet, in that brief period of time, it serves to validate the employee's work and leaves a lasting impression of interest on the part of the manager. If you really want to drive home the impact of the moment, you could follow up with a note or e-mail to HR for the employee's file. In addition, you should note it in your own file for reference when it comes time for the employee's review.

Experts agree that managers should coach often and be generous with praise; it doesn't cost anything, and the rewards can be enormous.

Performance-Improvement Spontaneous Coaching

Spontaneous coaching is equally effective when the focus is on performance improvement. While many managers find it daunting to provide corrective feedback, it can be helpful to remember that coaching involves an individual's performance—not his or her personality. The key to success is to share specific observations leading to a discussion of alternative behaviors or approaches, rather than merely pointing out what's wrong.

Suppose you're a manager in charge of customer service, and you overhear one of your representatives speaking curtly with a customer. While it may be tempting to issue a reprimand for inappropriate conduct, this will likely serve only to make the employee angry and resentful at having been "caught." Instead, you can view the unfortunate incident as an opportunity to engage in a dialog with the employee about what happened and how the matter might have been handled more effectively. Care must be taken not to lecture or come across as heavy-handed. Consider this exchange between Gwen, a customer service manager, and Vanessa, one of her representatives: Gwen has just walked by Vanessa's desk and heard the tail end of Vanessa's side of a phone conversation with a customer:

Vanessa: I don't know what else you want me to say! I'm sorry your order wasn't filled on time, but there's nothing I can do about it. The person you need to speak with is gone for the day. I'll tell him to call you tomorrow. That's the best I can do!"

Gwen: Sounds like you're having a rough time. What was that about?

Vanessa: That woman was so nasty! She started yelling at me and threatening to cancel her account with us because her delivery didn't arrive on time.

Gwen: I heard the last thing you said to her; I'm guessing she's still pretty upset. I know that some customers are harder to deal with than others, but here in customer service we always have to try to end on a positive note. Can you think of anything you might have said to her that would have accomplished that goal?

Vanessa: Not really; I don't like being yelled at and told I'm uncooperative.

Gwen: I guess not, but I wonder if she was really mad at *you* or frustrated over not having her order on time.

Vanessa: She doesn't know me, and I didn't do anything to her, so I guess she was just venting.

Gwen: And?

Vanessa: Well, I guess I could have told her I understand how upset she feels and that I'll do all that I can to help.

Gwen: Do you hear how your tone of voice just changed as soon as you acknowledged that she wasn't mad at *you*, personally? That enabled you to take a step back and assess the situation. I'll bet you've been in her shoes and just wanted to blow off steam.

Vanessa: True.

Gwen: Can you think of any way that you can smooth things over with the customer?

Vanessa: I guess I could call her back and say I want to verify the details of a memo I'm sending to the person who'll be calling her tomorrow.

Gwen: I think that's an excellent idea. And if you use the tone of voice you're using with me right now, I'm pretty sure she won't find you uncooperative.

This sort of exchange clearly takes more time and effort than the previous example of positive spontaneous coaching. It is well worth the effort, however, since employees are likely to come away understanding that you are interested in their performance. As a result, negative behavior is often replaced by constructive conduct.

> **• TIP #8 •**
>
> Spontaneous coaching requires you to be attentive and attuned to each employee's individual work habits, routines, and current assignments. This principle pertains to both positive and negative performance.

Planned Coaching

Spontaneous coaching is not always feasible or desirable. For example, if you observe a situation that calls for performance-improvement coaching, but there are other people around, it's best to wait until you and the employee are alone. However, you don't want to wait too long before addressing an issue that requires attention. Here's where planned coaching comes into play.

Planned coaching allows you to seek out an opportune time

to focus on a situation, but it is still informal in terms of the approach. For example, Steve, a store manager, observes one of his employees, Angie, talking on her cell phone while at the check-out register. He further observes a customer asking Angie a question, whereupon she holds up her index finger and mouths, "Hold on a minute; I'll be right with you." She finishes her personal call and then turns to the customer. Steve notes that the customer doesn't *seem* bothered, but Steve is. Her actions are inappropriate, and he needs to talk with Angie about the matter, but not in front of customers. He waits until Angie leaves the register for a break and then approaches her. "Angie, I need to speak with you in private for a moment," he states. They go into the cafeteria and find a table separate from the three other people in the room. He begins by making it clear that he knows for a fact that Angie was on the phone: "Angie, while you were at the cash register, you were also on your cell phone." He continues, "Do you feel you were able to focus fully on your customers while on the phone?" If Angie answers, "No," Steve can concur; if she says, "Yes," Steve can respond by saying, "Even if that's the case, customers may perceive you as being preoccupied and will therefore be less likely to ask questions. Perhaps some will even consider your behavior rude and will hesitate to come back." At this point, Steve should allow Angie to respond. She may say that she had an emergency, or perhaps she didn't think there was a problem. Regardless of what she says, Steve needs to listen. Then he should have her agree that talking on her cell phone while at the register is unacceptable and that she will not do it again.

This exchange should not take more than a couple of minutes. The discussion is not intended to be a reprimand, and Steve should allow Angie to extend her break time by the amount of time it took to talk with her. The matter is important and calls for immediate attention, but it is not grave.

• TIP #9 •

Planned coaching allows you to seek out an opportune time to focus on a situation, but it is still informal in terms of the approach.

3

Managers as Counselors

Counseling is the structured interaction between managers and their employees, with a keener focus on specific work-related problems. Its primary goal is to help employees achieve a maximum level of productivity in accordance with specified job duties, policies, and procedures. The process enables employees to examine their behavior, explore alternative ways of performing, and review the possible consequences of each alternative. In those instances when counseling proves insufficient, it may serve as a prelude to progressive disciplinary action.

To illustrate, let's return to the scenario between Steve and Angie. As you recall, Steve overheard Angie speaking on her cell phone while helping a customer. He spoke with her briefly, making clear that her behavior was unacceptable. Let's assume Angie agreed and committed to not making or receiving personal calls during working hours. Three weeks pass since the initial incident. Late one afternoon, Steve is once again in the store and witnesses Angie on the phone while at the register. Her voice is loud, making it clear that the conversation is of a personal, non-urgent, nature. When Angie sees Steve, she quickly ends the call. Steve quietly comments, "Angie, I thought we had an understanding about this." She nods, seemingly in agreement. Steve returns to the store a few days later, believing the matter with Angie has been resolved. Unfortunately, as he approaches Angie's register, he overhears her on the phone. Her tone is more hushed, but it's obvious she's talking with a friend and making plans for after work. Steve knows that the matter now requires formal counseling.

> **• TIP #10 •**
>
> Counseling is the structured interaction between managers and their employees, with a keener focus on specific work-related problems.

Counseling Characteristics

Just as coaching has a specific set of characteristics, so too does counseling:

Attentiveness

Whether spontaneous or planned, positive or improvement-oriented, your performance-appraisal responsibilities do not end with coaching. You cannot assume that productive behavior will prevail or that a word to the wise is enough to turn around a worker's poor work habits. Coaching is simply not always sufficient, and the attentive manager knows to be ever vigilant for changes in performance and attitude.

Sometimes these changes are subtle, impacting intangible aspects of an employee's work; for example, an otherwise outstanding employee seems a bit short-tempered whenever someone asks him a question. In other instances, the changes are quantifiable and more overt. Consider the employee who was able to meet his weekly deadlines after you coached him but has now reverted to turning in work a day late. In both cases, by being attentive, managers may follow-up coaching with more structured counseling.

Broad-Mindedness

Regardless of the jobs they perform, the nature of the work, or level of responsibility, every employee's performance affects others. If a worker is repeatedly late, his coworkers may have to pitch in, performing his work as well as their own until he arrives. This not only creates more work for them but also generates hard feelings and impacts relations amongst the workers, as well as between you and your employees. These motivational issues may ultimately result in reduced productivity.

For this reason, you cannot look the other way when an employee's behavior is outside the parameters of her job. By being broad-minded, you can leverage the impact one employee's behavior has on others.

Commitment

Savvy managers know that being committed to helping employees achieve a maximum level of productivity in accordance with specified job duties, policies, and procedures can be highly beneficial to all concerned. Here are some of the positive outcomes that can result from displaying commitment: Employees are likely to respond favorably, both in attitude and behavior, to your efforts; your level of self-confidence is elevated upon seeing the results of your efforts; others within and outside the department, aware of the productive working relationship between you and your workers, seek to duplicate it; and productivity throughout the organization can improve.

Conscientiousness

You need to be ever vigilant about what's going on in your department. Whether it concerns an individual employee in relation to her job, a matter between you and an employee, or an issue concerning two or more employees, your degree of conscientiousness is directly related to the extent of your effectiveness in matters concerning counseling. Even if everything appears to be proceeding smoothly, it is still prudent for you to determine, firsthand, the status of what each employee is working on, as well as any interpersonal matters that could impact work. Then, if anything is out of sync, you can step in with counseling.

Focus

It's easy for first-time managers to become sidetracked when it comes to matters impacting employee performance, but with a little effort you can remain focused and make objective decisions. Here's an example that illustrates this point: Let's say you have three people reporting to you, all performing a similar function. Tina has been an exemplary employee for two years; Marcus, hired ten months ago, is performing competently; and Kathryn, on board for just eight weeks, is still learning the job, but shows promise. Kathryn and Marcus begin to see one another outside of work. Soon, it becomes evident that they are romantically involved, although their behavior in the office remains professional. Tina comes to you and says she's uneasy knowing that her colleagues are dating, claiming that it makes her feel like an "outsider." She maintains that she's having trouble concentrating and demands that you make them stop.

As you reflect on what Tina is saying, you acknowledge that Tina's work has, indeed, fallen below par over the past few weeks. However, while you understand her point of view and you would not want her to become so unhappy as to quit, you focus on the facts: (1) there is no policy saying employees cannot date; (2) neither Kathryn's nor Marcus's work has suffered as a result of their dating; (3) they have both exhibited the same professional behavior as before they began dating; (4) there have not been any other complaints aside from Tina's; (5) there is no way to determine, absolutely, that Tina's decline in performance is related to Kathryn and Marcus. By focusing on the facts in this matter, it's evident that you need to deal with Tina's issues separately and apart from Kathryn and Marcus.

Interest

Maintaining an active interest in your employees is likely to result in a good rapport. Then, should counseling issues develop, employees are likely to be more responsive and less resentful. Note that interest does not mean involvement. For example, Theresa is distraught because she's struggling with a class she's taking after work at the local community college. She confides in Mike, her manager, describing the difficult course content. Mike replies, "I remember taking that class; I did really well in it!" Upon hearing this, Theresa is hopeful that Mike will help her prepare for her final. At this point, Mike needs to remind himself that he can maintain interest without getting personally involved. Therefore, an appropriate response would be: "Theresa, I'm confident that you'll do well on your own. If you feel you need help, I'm sure your professor will offer assistance, or you might consider joining a study group. In fact, that's just what I did."

Realism

If you're a first-time manager who has come up through the ranks, you might be in charge of employees performing your old job. Assuming you executed your tasks in an exemplary manner, it's hard for you not to expect others to do so as well. Still, it's important that you take into account each individual's level of skill, degree of knowledge, and extent of interest in relation to the expectations of the job, rather than your personal expectations based on your own prior level of performance. Approaching each employee realistically will allow you to assess your human resources objectively in relation to achieving departmental goals, as well as helping each worker achieve his or her personal goals. Should counseling be necessary, you will have a clearer sense of what he or she needs to accomplish.

• TIP #11 •

To be effective in your role as a counselor, strive to be attentive, broad-minded, committed, conscientious, focused, interested, and realistic.

Directive Counseling

The directive-counseling approach requires you to identify the problem, tell the employee why it's a problem, and then tell the employee what he or she needs to do to rectify the matter. You will probably also want to include a detailed timeline. The communication is pretty much one-way, including what you've identified as specific consequences for inappropriate behavior.

Here's an example of directive counseling that might follow the planned coaching exchange between Angie and Steve:

"Angie, I called you in here to discuss the use of your cell phone for personal calls during working hours. As you recall, I spoke with you about this three weeks ago; since that time, I've personally overheard you on your phone with customers nearby on three separate occasions. This behavior is in direct violation of store policy and must stop immediately. If you have to make a personal phone call, I expect you to do so during breaks or lunch. I need you to comply immediately. If I catch you on the phone again I will be forced to begin disciplinary proceedings and write you up."

By using a directive-counseling approach, managers are in complete control, steering the method for resolving the employee's problem. Notice the repetitive use of the pronoun "I" in Steve's monologue. Practitioners of directive counseling tell and advise, asserting that they have answers that will help the employee get back on track.

Since this technique leaves little room for dispute or confusion, it may initially appear to ensure a positive outcome; unfortunately, it rarely does. In fact, the directive-counseling approach often results in damaged employer-employee relations, often reaching a point of nonrepair. To make matters worse, the impact of the tainted manager/employee relationship frequently spills over into the workplace, creating disharmony amongst other workers and ultimately impacting productivity. This happens because employees typically resent being told they have a problem and further resent being told how to solve it, even if the advice is sound.

• TIP #12 •

The directive-counseling approach requires you to identify the problem, tell the employee why it's a problem, and then tell the employee what he or she needs to do to rectify the matter. This approach rarely achieves the desired outcome.

Nondirective Counseling

The nondirective-counseling approach calls for a partnership between you and your employees, with each having a specified role. While it is more structured than the directive-counseling approach, it is far less rigid in its application. Experts believe that the nondirective approach is more likely to result in positive change because the employee has greater control over his or her behavior. The sequence of nondirective counseling steps is as follows:

Step One: You begin by stating the purpose of the counseling session. Forexample, "Angie, I called you in here to discuss the use of your cell phone for personal calls during working hours." This introductory statement is identical to that used to illustrate the directive approach.

Step Two: You then define and recap the problem: "As you recall, I spoke with you about this three weeks ago; since that time, I have personally overheard you on your phone with customers nearby on three separate occasions." Again, the language is the same as that used in the directive-approach example. Similarities between the two counseling methods are about to change, however.

Step Three: The next step calls for you to identify the company policy or rule that the employee has violated. With the directive approach, Steve began by saying, "This behavior is in direct violation of store policy and must stop immediately."

Here's where we begin to see a distinction between the two forms of counseling.

Using the nondirective approach, Steve would first cite the specific policy that Angie has violated: "Angie, on page 27 of your employee handbook, it states that employees are not permitted to make or receive personal calls during working hours, except in the event of an emergency." He would then continue by adding, "The 'Phone Use' section of your handbook explains that employees may make personal calls during breaks or on their lunch hour."

By referencing a specific portion of the employee hand-book, rather than making a vague reference to some policy, Steve draws Angie's focus to something tangible and impersonal, making it more difficult for her to become defensive over a policy she is expected to know about.

Step Four: Now it's the employee's turn to express her take on the situation. In the scenario between Steve and Angie, Steve could turn to Angie and simply state, "I'd like to hear what you have to say about this." She might respond with "I really don't see why this is a problem. I'm perfectly capable of talking on the phone while working the register. Have any of the customers complained? Have I made any mistakes? I don't get why this is a big deal."

What should follow is a dialogue between you and the employee. It's important that you remain objective throughout this exchange, adhering to the facts, the content of the policy violated, and the impact of the violation on the workplace. The employee should be encouraged to express her views, as long as the discussion doesn't escalate into an argument. When it appears that both parties have expressed themselves, it's time to move on to step 5.

Step Five: At this point you need to clarify and restate the problem, as well as acknowledge the employee's perspective. Hence, Steve might say, "Angie, I understand you feel strongly about being able to talk on the phone while doing your job without error or complaint. It may very well be that you can; however, the fact remains that the store has a specific policy about using the phone during working hours, and everyone needs to adhere to it."

You should remain objective and not reference your personal feelings. The directive-counseling approach, on the other hand, had Steve repeatedly making "I" statements: "*I* expect you to do so during breaks or lunch. *I* need you to comply immediately. If *I* catch you on the phone again, *I* will be forced to write you up."

Step Six: Now it's time to come up with a viable solution to the problem. The responsibility for this falls on the shoulders of the employee, although you are responsible for dismissing those solutions that are unworkable. For example, an employee with a chronic punctuality problem may suggest that she be permitted to start work one hour later. If flextime is not offered in your organization, then this is not a viable option. You are also responsible for ultimately approving the approach selected by the employee. This stage of the nondirective approach to counseling, then, is a joint effort between you and the employee.

To illustrate by way of the scenario between Angie and Steve, Angie might say, "I can't say that I agree with the policy about personal phone calls, but I guess I'll just have to comply; I'll try to make my calls during lunch or breaks. But you have to understand—sometimes my mom calls when I'm at the register, and since she's been in and out of the hospital lately, I need to make sure she's all right." Steve might reply, "How about this: Explain to your mom that you can't talk during working hours, unless it's an urgent situation. That way, if she does call, you'll know it's pressing. We can certainly show flexibility in the event of an emergency. Now, what can you do about other incoming phone calls?" Angie thinks for a moment, then replies: "Well, I guess I can keep my phone on mute and check it every once in awhile to see if my mom or anyone else has called; if it's a friend I can call them back during breaks or lunch. Is that good?" Steve smiles and says, "Yes, Angie, that sounds like a viable solution. Let's meet again in a week to talk about how it's going."

Step Seven: The final stage of nondirective counseling is the follow-up. Depending on the nature of the infraction, you should arrange to meet with employees after they have had a chance to implement agreed-upon changes, generally in one to two weeks. If needed, they can agree on additional, subsequent checkpoint dates.

> ### • TIP #13 •
>
> The nondirective-counseling approach calls for a partnership be-tween you and your employees, with each having a specified role. Because the employee has greater control over her own behavior, the nondirective approach is more likely to result in positive change.

• 4 •

The Golden Rules of Performance Appraisals

Witness the contrast between two new managers, each of whom is about to conduct a performance review for the first time. Ted views the process as overwhelming and fraught with pitfalls. He's attended a workshop and read several books on the subject, none of which has alleviated his high level of anxiety. Despite all that he's learned, he worries that he'll make mistakes. What if he says the wrong thing? How should he communicate that the employee has been performing poorly? What if he has nothing whatsoever to say that's positive? Should he bring up past mistakes the employee has made? Won't that upset the employee and taint the climate of the meeting? And what about the superstar in his department—how does he offer suggestions for ongoing development when she performs her job better than he does his?

His colleague, Francesca, has a completely different take on performance appraisals and finds Ted's concerns amusing. She, too, has to conduct an appraisal on a poor performer and agrees wholeheartedly that preparation is crucial to a successful meeting; but she doesn't worry that the employee is going to react with surprise or dismay upon learning that he has not been performing in a satisfactory manner because he's already aware of how he's doing. She also knows there's always room for additional growth, so offering suggestions to a worker whose performance is wonderful doesn't stress her out one bit.

Francesca understands that ongoing coaching and counseling set the stage for any performance review; that is, by doing her job as an effective coach and counselor, she'll be prepared to successfully apply the three golden rules of performance appraisal: (1) nothing that is ever said during a performance appraisal meeting should come as a surprise to the employee; (2) managers should be prepared to praise and criticize elements of the employee's work from the time of the employee's last review or date of hire; and (3) every incident that is referenced should be documented.

Let's see how following these golden rules can help you conduct maximally effective performance appraisals.

• TIP #14 •

Ongoing coaching and counseling set the stage for the performance-review meeting; that is, by doing your job as an effective coach and counselor, you will be prepared to apply successfully the three golden rules of performance appraisal.

This Should Come as No Surprise . . .

When employees enter your office for the annual performance review, they should have a clear sense of how they're going to be evaluated. If they've consistently been doing well, they should know this as a result of informal, ongoing praise offered by you throughout the year (coaching); if there have been performance-related problems, they will be already be aware of these problems as a result of more structured sessions (counseling).

To illustrate, we'll return to the coaching offered by Gwen to Vanessa, a customer service representative, in Chapter 2, and the counseling provided by Steve to Angie, a sales associate, in Chapter 3. Several months have passed in each scenario, and it's now time for their respective annual performance reviews. Let's begin with Gwen and Vanessa:

As you recall, Gwen was walking by Vanessa's desk when she overheard the tail end of Vanessa's side of a phone conversation with a customer. Vanessa was clearly agitated with what she perceived to be the customer's unreasonable demands and made clear her feelings to the customer. Gwen spoke with her immediately after the incident, and Vanessa acknowledged that she could have been more tactful in her approach. In addition, she offered to rectify the matter by following up with the customer the next day. During the portion of Vanessa's performance appraisal pertaining to challenging customer service issues, Gwen should raise the matter of Vanessa's handling of that customer, but not as a focal point involving criticism; rather, she should refer to it as an example of how she effectively converted negative behavior into a positive outcome. It becomes a recap rather than a new topic. More significantly, it becomes a positive reference, setting the tone for the rest of the review.

The matter concerning Angie is more complicated: What started out as coaching on Steve's part escalated into counseling. Let's assume that Steve opted for the nondirective method of counseling. Let us further assume that he last spoke with Angie about her inappropriate use of the phone during working hours three months prior to her annual performance appraisal and that there have been no additional incidents since that time. At some point during Angie's performance appraisal meeting, Steve will raise the matter of her phone use, but not to chastise her. He will review what happened, identify the steps she took toward preventing the matter from occurring again, and commend her on successfully resolving the matter.

But what if the matter concerning her inappropriate phone use remains unresolved by the time of her performance appraisal meeting? Steve now needs to take a different approach. He will review the steps taken to date, and then comment on the impact of Angie's failure to amend her behavior on her overall evaluation.

In both of these scenarios, the employees are well aware of

the issues concerning their performance prior to meeting for their annual reviews: Angie knows that she violated company policy on more than one occasion by talking on her cell phone during working hours, and Vanessa knows that Gwen disapproved of how she responded to a customer.

• TIP #15 •

Golden Rule #1:

Nothing that is said during a performance appraisal should ever come as a surprise to an employee.

Praise and Criticism

The second golden rule of performance appraisals is that you should always strive to include both praise and criticism during the review process. This can be more difficult than one might initially think, even when it comes to employees who perform exceedingly well. Consider Taylor, who performs every task in an outstanding fashion. As a payroll clerk, she performs her job efficiently and meticulously, is always on time, stays after hours to help others meet their deadlines, and even volunteers to take on additional work. Not only that, she's also pleasant to be around. What is there to criticize? Should you make something up just to strike a balance or keep her from getting a big head? No, of course not. What you need to realize is that criticism is not necessarily a negative observation concerning poor performance; rather, it can entail noting an area that, if improved upon, will likely make the person's work that much better.

Let's take a closer look at Taylor's performance. While clearly an excellent worker, her manager, Maggie, has noticed that Taylor often checks her work multiple times before submitting it, as well as asking someone else to look it over. While it's hard to criticize her for being so focused on the quality of her work, Maggie wonders whether Taylor doesn't lack sufficient self-confidence. As she prepares for Taylor's annual review,

Maggie considers how she'll broach the subject. Here's one possible approach: "Taylor, after reviewing each category on the appraisal form, there's no question that your overall work is 'outstanding:' That's the highest possible rating you can achieve. Before we turn our attention to your goals for the upcoming year, however, I'd like to talk with you about how you approach one aspect of your work. I've noticed that you check over your numbers several times and also ask others to review your work prior to submission. While I appreciate your commitment to accuracy, I wonder whether you need to devote quite so much time to this. I'm confident that you can achieve the same level of accuracy without being that methodical. In fact, I'd like to see you devote the time you'd save to pursuing other areas of responsibility and interest. Let's talk about what some of those areas might include."

Now, let's consider balancing criticism with praise. Unfortunately, despite a manager's coaching and counseling efforts throughout the year, some employees continue to exhibit poor performance. Without improvement, it's hard not to focus on their shortcomings during the appraisal process; its harder still, to identify positive traits. Here's my take on this: If they're so awful that there's absolutely nothing good to say about them, then they shouldn't be on the payroll. If they are, then there's got to be something they're doing right. Figure out what that something is, isolate it, and see whether there's something inherent in that trait that can help get the person back on track. Remember that the primary objective of a performance appraisal is to ensure the maximum utilization of every employee's skills, knowledge, and interests. That includes marginal performers—at least until such time as their performance is so bad as to warrant termination.

To illustrate, meet Jack, who worked successfully as a teller in a small, suburban branch of a bank until eight months ago, at which time he was transferred to one of the larger branches in the city. The adjustment has been difficult for Jack, resulting in numerous mistakes and customer complaints about how long it takes him to complete transactions. Initially, Jack's manager, Allie, thought the logical solution was to send him back to the suburbs, but Jack had moved into the city and couldn't manage so long a commute. Allie offered coaching, then counseling, but to no avail. Jack just didn't seem to be able to handle the high volume of customers and impatience they exhibited, especially during the busy lunch hour. Jack also missed knowing his customers by name and exchanging small talk with his "regulars."

Allie thought about all of this when it came time for his review. She tried hard to concentrate on Jack's strengths and, after some thought, concluded that Jack clearly possessed good interpersonal skills. Allie decided, therefore, to focus on a way to build on that strength.

During his review, Allie began, "Jack, over the past several months we've talked at length about the trouble you're having on the job. Right now, I'd like to talk about what you do well; that is, how capable you are of dealing with bank customers when time permits. Unfortunately, unlike your other location, this branch is a high-pressure environment, calling for quick turnaround. So, what I'd us to do is explore, together, ways in which you might be able to apply your interpersonal skills more successfully in your current work environment."

> ### • TIP #16 •
>
> *Golden Rule #2:*
>
> Always strive to include both praise and constructive criticism when conducting performance appraisals.

Documentation

The third golden rule of performance appraisals is to document every incident referenced. As you perform your coaching and counseling roles, be diligent about documenting all related exchanges. Unlike documenting the steps in a disciplinary proceeding, these notes need not follow a strict protocol; rather, they are meant to serve as a refresher, for both manager and employee, of why the conversation took place, what was discussed, and what, if anything, was agreed upon. Dating this notation and keeping it in an "Employee Performance Log" allows you to readily access and add to the running commentary of coaching and counseling occurrences involving all of your employees.

Here's a sample format:

• Employee Performance Log •

Date _____

Name _____ *Title* _____

Coaching _____ *Counseling* _____

Why I Coached/Counseled This Employee:

_____
_____
_____

Who Said What:

_____
_____
_____

Who Agreed to Do What and by When:

_____
_____
_____

As you can see, this is a fairly informal set-up, allowing a lot of latitude for each manager to fill in the information as he sees fit. Entering this or a similar form onto your computer is probably the easiest approach. Arrange the information by employee, function, date, or any other way that works best for you.

The information in this log will prove invaluable when it comes time for the employee's formal performance appraisal. You won't have to rely on your memory to recall specific performance-related incidences, and employees won't be caught off guard, hearing about incidents for the first time. Just as importantly, the information in the log will serve as an indisputable foundation of fact, allowing both the manager and employee to move forward in a positive direction.

Here's an example using an Employee Performance Log to record what has taken place between Angie and Steve in the months leading up to Angie's performance review:

• Employee Performance Log •

Date: January 23, 2XXX

Name: Angie _____   *Title:* Sales Associate _____

Coaching: ___√___ *Counseling* _____

Why I Coached/Counseled This Employee:
Observed Angie talking on her cell phone while at the checkout register; customer waiting to be helped. _____

Who Said What:
I told Angie that I saw her on her cell phone; asked her whether she felt she could focus fully on her customers while on the phone; she said, "Yes." I said that customers may perceive her as being preoccupied or rude, and I added that it was unacceptable behavior. _____

Who Agreed to Do What and by When:
Angie said she didn't think it was a problem but agreed she wouldn't do it again. _____

• Employee Performance Log •

Date: February 15, 2XXX

Name: Angie _____   *Title:* Sales Associate _____

Coaching: ___√___ *Counseling* _____

Why I Coached/Counseled This Employee:
Observed Angie once again talking on her cell phone while at the register. _____

Who Said What:
When I passed Angie at the register while she was on her cell phone she quickly hung up. I said, "Angie, I thought we had an understanding about this." She nodded. _____

Who Agreed to Do What and by When:
There was no discussion. I thought we had an agreement when we
spoke three weeks ago.

• Employee Performance Log •

Date: February 22, 2XXX

Name: Angie   *Title:* Sales Associate

Coaching: _____   *Counseling* _____

Why I Coached/Counseled This Employee:
I observed Angie once again on her cell phone while at the register. Did
not comment; do not know whether she saw me. Decision: I will have
to counsel her about this.

Who Said What:
N/A

Who Agreed to Do What and by When:
N/A

• Employee Performance Log •

Date: February 24, 2XXX

Name: Angie   *Title:* Sales Associate

Coaching: _____   *Counseling* __√__

Why I Coached/Counseled This Employee:
I witnessed Angie using her cell phone while at the register on three
separate occasions. She agreed to stop after the first incident (see
coaching notes).

Who Said What:
I recapped our previous discussions about the inappropriate use of her
cell phone, as well as what I'd witnessed. I reminded Angie of the
company policy concerning personal phone calls during working hours
(reference: page 27 of the employee handbook). Angie said she doesn't
see why this is a problem and that she can talk on the phone while
working the register. I explained that the policy on this matter is clear
and that customers are entitled to expect undivided attention when
checking out. Furthermore, all employees are expected to comply.

Who Agreed to Do What and by When:
Angie maintained that she doesn't agree with the policy but that she
would comply, adding that she'd try to make calls during lunch or
breaks. If calls come in from her mother, who is ill, we agreed to make
an exception. Angie will keep her phone on mute and check it every
once in awhile to see whether her mom has called. We agreed to follow
up in a week.

• Employee Performance Log •

Date: March 2, 2XXX

Name: Angie   *Title:* Sales Associate

Coaching: _____   *Counseling Follow-up:* __√__

Why I Coached/Counseled/Followed-Up With This Employee:
No further incidents involving Angie's use of the cell phone since
counseling session.

Who Said What:
I asked Angie how it was going; she said she's adjusted to not using her
cell phone while on the register.

Who Agreed to Do What and by When:
Angie agreed to continue to comply.

• Tip #17 •

Golden Rule #3:

Document every incident that is referenced in a performance appraisal.

· 5 ·

Gathering Information

First-time managers often wonder whether their employee evaluations are based on sufficient objective information to be considered accurate. After all, rarely do you see your workers all the time; more often, you just see the end result, missing out on the effort that goes into the process.

Evaluating an employee's performance is, indeed, a huge responsibility and, as such, shouldn't be shouldered by any one person. Accordingly, an important aspect of getting ready for the appraisal meeting is gathering information from several sources. You can then compare their personal observations concerning the employee's accomplishments, areas requiring improvement, and success in meeting previously set goals with those of others with whom the employee works or interacts. In addition, you can ask the employee to conduct a self-evaluation. You should also measure actual performance against predetermined standards of performance as set forth in the job description.

· TIP #18 ·

An important aspect of getting ready for the appraisal meeting is gathering and comparing information from several sources.

Job Descriptions

You can't very well determine whether an employee is performing well without something tangible against which to measure his performance. Before conducting appraisals, you need to review those qualifications that are necessary to do a job, and clearly identify the specific tasks that employees are expected to perform. This is best accomplished in the form of a job description.

Job descriptions have two primary purposes: to identify the essential functions of a job, and to clarify what the incumbent is expected to accomplish. Effectively, then, job descriptions form the groundwork for an informal agreement between an employer and an employee as to expected job-performance results.

Job Requirements

Job requirements are position-specific educational and prior experience prerequisites. In other words, they're a way of identifying the skills and knowledge that are necessary to perform the primary duties and responsibilities of a job successfully.

All educational and prior experience requirements should accurately and realistically reflect the level and nature of the position. In addition, these requirements should be able to stand up under legal scrutiny. *Consider:* requiring a college degree or even a high-school diploma may get you into legal hot water if you cannot show that someone without the degree or diploma could successfully perform the essential functions of a job. In addition, an educational prerequisite may produce a person who attended and graduated from school, but it does not, in and of itself, reflect what that person learned or is capable of doing.

When it comes to prior experience, be sure to identify that which is both tangible and intangible. *Examples of tangible experience requirements include:* demonstrated ability to lift cartons weighing 20–40 pounds; proven track record of increasing monthly sales; and substantial experience in preparing annual budget reports. *Examples of intangible experience requirements in-*

clude: "evidence of ability to establish and maintain rapport with coworkers"; "proven ability to communicate successfully with attendees of training programs"; and "demonstrated skill in negotiating."

Duties and Responsibilities

Job descriptions typically list duties and responsibilities in a logical, sequential order, beginning with the task requiring the greatest amount of time or carrying the most responsibility. Action words are used to help convey to the reader a degree of responsibility. *For example,* compare "directs" with "under the direction of."

Maximum effectiveness can be achieved if the language conveys the purpose behind the task. Compare the following statements: Statement A: "Maintains data on departmental transactions; prepares reports as needed." *Statement B:* "Maintains data on departmental transactions concerning the projected expansion; prepares and submits reports needed for long-term organizational forecasting to members of senior management."

Statement A reflects language from a standard list-approach to writing job descriptions. It is accurate and descriptive and uses action words ("maintains" and "prepares"); however, it is incomplete in that it fails to clarify what the incumbent is expected to accomplish. When it comes time to conduct a performance appraisal, *Statement B* better defines the task and the purpose behind it, thereby allowing for an evaluation of how successful the employee has been in performing that specific task.

Using the Job Description as a Reference Point

For greatest accuracy and efficiency, managers can simply reference the job description for each category on the appraisal form. For example, let's assume that one of the categories on the performance appraisal form is "Decision Making." The manager can now refer to the employee's job description and see that it calls for the ability to "identify both existing and potential departmental problems, and to develop steps or procedures to resolve these problems." The manager now looks at the possible ratings: *Far exceeds* the requirements of the job; *exceeds* the requirements of the job; *meets* the requirements of the job; *occasionally meets* the requirements of the job; *fails to meet* the requirements of the job. Guided by specific instances in which the employee engaged in decision making, the manager can select and objectively support the most suitable rating.

In doing this for each category, managers can be assured that they are objectively measuring performance against job-specific criteria.

> **• TIP #19 •**
>
> Before conducting appraisals, review those qualifications that are necessary to do a job, and clearly identify the specific tasks that employees are expected to perform. This is best accomplished in the form of a job description.

360-Degree Evaluation

With the 360-degree evaluation method, performance input is received from several sources. This is done to ensure a well-rounded appraisal and to enhance employee development and growth. This method was originally developed to help evaluate managers; it has since evolved into a tool that is frequently used for all employees. In particular, organizations see it as a way to enhance teamwork.

Employees may be rated by any of a number of individuals with whom they have contact. This often includes officers and administrators, managers other than their own, peers and associates, direct reports, clients, customers, consultants, and outside vendors, according to predetermined job-specific competencies. The actual number of feedback sources considered desirable varies from organization to organization, depending largely on the level and impact of the position.

In many instances, everyone is asked to complete the same

form so all concerned are evaluating the same competencies. Sometimes, though, the process is less structured, and feedback is provided by way of casual comments. The results are used for comparative evaluative purposes; rarely is this feedback used to determine salary adjustments or changes in job status.

The identities of reviewers are usually kept confidential. This anonymity is believed to increase the tendencies of evaluators to provide honest feedback, thereby affording the employee being rated a more accurate assessment of strengths and areas requiring improvement.

Consider this 360-degree evaluation scenario: One month before meeting with Luke, a marketing associate, Lorrie, his manager, considers the various individuals with whom he regularly comes in contact. She narrows the field to five people whom she believes can provide input regarding Luke's work performance over the past year: Rhonda, Luke's coworker; Eric, the secretary in the marketing department; and representatives from three major companies to whom Luke regularly provides services. Lorrie is especially interested in learning their views concerning Luke's success in communicating information as it relates to new marketing plans. She asks each person to rate Luke according to the organization's four evaluation categories of "outstanding," "very good," "fair," and "poor," as well as to provide an example to support their respective evaluations. Here's what she receives back:

- *From Rhonda:* "Luke clearly deserves a rating of 'outstanding.' He's constantly sharing his ideas about new marketing plans. The last one he pitched—the one involving multiple overlays—was ingenious. Of course, I don't have to tell you that; the campaign earned the company big bucks!"

- *From Eric:* "I'd give Luke a really high evaluation. He's incredibly smart, although he isn't always clear about what he wants me to do—like the project involving multiple overlays. I had to go to him several times and in the end just guessed at what he wanted."

- *From Client #1:* "Luke is excellent; that is to say, outstanding. He manages to convince me to take a risk and step outside of our past marketing strategies; he's always right on target."
- *From Client #2:* "Luke is reliable and consistent. He's very, very good at what he does. Each project is better than the one before."
- *From Client #3:* "Outstanding; especially the way he presented the idea of using multiple overlays."

The information provided through this 360-degree approach helps Lorrie prepare for her evaluation of Luke. Based on the feedback she's received, coupled with her own observations, Lorrie is comfortable giving Luke a rating of "outstanding" when it comes to communicating information relative to new marketing plans.

Sometimes there's conflicting input from one or more sources. For instance, if one of Luke's clients said that Luke missed the mark when it came to understanding it's needs, yet all the other feedback suggested otherwise, you would need to explore to determine the basis for the discrepancy. Could there have been an interpersonal clash? Perhaps there was miscommunication in terms of the desired end. Majority does not always rule, but generally if four out of five individuals rate an employee's work similarly, there should be a sound basis for it.

• TIP #20 •

With the 360-degree method of appraisal, performance input is received from the manager as well as several additional sources. This is done to provide a well-rounded evaluation and to enhance employee development and growth.

Self-Appraisals

Increasingly, employers are asking employees to conduct self-appraisals to supplement the manager's evaluation. Indeed, self-appraisals may be part of the 360-degree evaluation method. This process allows employees to compare their own assessments with those of their managers, and vice versa. Employees may be asked to complete the same appraisal form as you, or to respond to isolated categories such as: perceived strengths and areas requiring improvement; areas in which greater experience and/or education is desired; aspects of their work environment that they find helpful; changes in their work environment that would help improve performance; aspects of their work that they enjoy and, conversely, dislike; additional projects or tasks they would like to work on; immediate goals; long-term career plans; and steps needed to achieve immediate and long-term goals.

Self-appraisals can enhance employer-employee relations if both parties remain open-minded and receptive to differing views.

Managers who have never asked employees to conduct self-appraisals often assume that the results will be glowing, with outstanding results in every category. Interestingly, this is not what generally happens, especially when employees are asked to provide supporting statements for their evaluations. Boasting about one's accomplishments can be difficult; providing specific examples can be even more challenging. Conversely, identifying areas requiring improvement can be made a more palatable assignment if concrete illustrations are called for.

To help employees prepare effective self-evaluations, you should schedule a meeting about a month prior to the face-to-face appraisal session. The following monologues illustrate some options as to how you can introduce the subject of self-appraisals to employees, using an evaluation form:

Option #1: "As you probably know, your annual performance review is coming up in about a month. I'm going to be completing the evaluation form and thought you'd like to do the same. Rate yourself for each category, and provide examples that support your ratings. Bring the completed form to our meeting, and we'll compare my assessment with your self-appraisals. If you have any questions about what any of the categories means, just call HR."

Option #2: "I'm going to be preparing for your annual performance review next month, and I'd like you to prepare a self-review prior to our meeting so I can see how you view your performance in various categories. Let's go over a blank form so I can be sure that you understand what's required."

Option #3: "As you know, Updon Industries values employee input; this philosophy extends to performance appraisals. I'm going to be filling out the appraisal form prior to our meeting on August 5th. I'd like you to do the same; that is, rate your own performance. You can either submit the completed form to me prior to our meeting or bring it with you on the fifth. Let's spend a few minutes going over the form to ensure that you understand what each rating means."

Some organizations opt for a less formal approach to self-appraisals; that is, they don't require employees to complete forms. Instead, in such cases, you may use one of the following approaches:

Option #1: "Next month is your annual review. Before we meet, I'd like you to give some thought to how you think you've done over the past year. Jot down some notes about where you feel you've excelled, as well as any areas in which you feel there's room for improvement. Then, when we meet, we'll compare your self-evaluation with how I've assessed your work."

Option #2: "Here are some questions I'd like you to take a look at. As you can see, they all have to do with your work performance over the past year. Could you get your answers to me about a week before we meet on August 5th? Don't let the questions about improvement throw you; if there are areas you think you need to work on, just say so."

Option #3: "I wanted to talk with you about your upcoming performance appraisal. I know it's still a month away, but I've already started thinking about how you've performed over the past year, and I'd like you to do the same. Here are some questions that tie in directly with the form I'll be completing. Don't be modest about your accomplishments; likewise, be frank if you see areas in which you feel you need to improve."

• TIP #21 •

Self-evaluations allow employees to compare their own assessments with those of their managers, and vice versa.

• 6 •

Preparing to Conduct Appraisals on Former Coworkers

Meet Tom, a first-time manager at a manufacturing plant in the Midwest. Up until the time of his promotion, Tom worked for two years "on the floor," along with his dad and several good friends. When the opportunity for a promotion to manager came along, Tom applied, hoping, but never believing, that he'd be selected. When he was told the good news, Tom had a mixed reaction: He was thrilled to be moving a step closer to his ultimate goal of department head, but the promotion also meant he was going to supervise his friends; more significantly, he was going to be in charge of his own father! Tom's dad joked about how his son was now his boss, but Tom wasn't amused; in fact, he was extremely uncomfortable, especially since annual reviews were rapidly approaching, and his dad had a chronic attendance problem. How was he supposed to tell his own father that he had to get to work on time or face disciplinary action?

Fortunately, Tom's situation is somewhat unique, but only insofar as managing his father is concerned. A lot can change when a former colleague becomes a manager, impacting every aspect of the relationship. The new "boss" isn't as likely to be invited to lunch "with the gang," or included in after-work social events. Former coworkers are careful when divulging office gossip or telling jokes involving managers. Some may resent the fact that you were selected over them; others will try to use your former relationship to garner favors. Ideally, there will also be those who are supportive and encouraging as you step into your new managerial role and this support will be extended to the review process.

Whether the support is there or not, you should clarify respective roles, establish expectations, and follow certain guidelines before attempting to review the work of former colleagues.

> ## • TIP #22 •
> A lot can change when a former coworker becomes a manager, impacting every aspect of the relationship. Before reviewing the work of former colleagues, you should clarify respective roles and establish expectations.

Clarify Respective Roles

The process of preparing to conduct appraisals on former coworkers begins with clarifying everyone's respective roles and responsibilities in the new manager-employee relationship. This clarification will impact all aspects of performance appraisals, including coaching and counseling.

Coaching

In Chapter 2, you learned that coaching is the day-to-day interaction between you and your employees, and that the goal of coaching is to regularly offer assistance, support, praise, and constructive criticism. You also learned of seven characteristics that you should strive to demonstrate in order to be maximally effective as coaches; that is, to be approachable, consistent, dependable, empathetic, honest, knowledgeable, and respectful. Applying these traits can be challenging enough without adding to the mix the awkwardness of having to manage former coworkers.

Let's reference three of these traits and corresponding examples from Chapter 2 as the basis for additional, productive dialogue between Sean, a recently promoted first-time manager, and Mike, his former colleague. As coworkers, Sean and Mike interacted amicably but were never what either would describe as friends. Despite extending good wishes for success, Mike has made it clear that he believes he should have been promoted instead of Sean.

Trait: *Approachability*

Sean: I know the Johnson report is taking more time than you'd originally anticipated. I just want you to know that I'm available if you want to use me as a sounding board and go over what remains to be done.

Mike: That's generous of you, buddy, especially since you're not the one who has to do it anymore.

Sean: I just wanted you to know that I'm here if you need me.

Rather than engaging in a discussion that will more than likely lead to an uncomfortable discussion about his promotion, Sean wisely opts to reiterate his original offer and leave it at that.

Trait: *Honesty*

Sean: Mike, despite the fact that you fell short of your overall goal of three new clients for the month, you exhibited tremendous effort.

Mike: What does that mean?

Sean: It means that you can probably meet your goal next month if you modify your approach somewhat.

Mike: And what happens if I don't? I mean, you were promoted for doing what you do, and obviously I wasn't, so, do I get demoted if I fail?

Sean: Let's focus on how you can meet your goal. What do you see yourself doing differently in order to generate three new accounts each month?

Mike's reaction to Sean's statements is contentious. Rather than taking the bait and arguing about who was promoted and why, Sean wisely steers clear by addressing the issue at hand: what Mike has to do in order to meet his goal.

Trait: *Respectfulness*

Sean: I'd like your input regarding how best to go about achieving results.

Mike: What's the matter, Sean? You don't want anyone to know that you can't do your new job? I've got to say, if I'd gotten the promotion I'd think twice about coming to you for help.

Sean: I know you enjoy a good challenge, Mike. That's why I'm coming to you.

Sean's response to Mike's taunting query is both professional and respectful. He could easily become defensive but instead chooses to make clear that by helping him, Mike is helping himself.

Counseling

As you learned in Chapter 3, managers are also responsible for counseling in those instances when work-related issues require a keener focus. You should strive to be attentive, broad-minded, committed, conscientious, focused, interested, and realistic in dealing with employee problems. This last trait—being realistic—can be especially challenging when it comes to managing the work you once performed yourself. Assuming that you executed your tasks in an exemplary manner, it's hard not to expect others to do the same. But not everyone performs at the same skill level, has the same degree of knowledge, or possesses the same level of interest. Managers of former coworkers need to be realistic about what each employee can and wants to do, especially if there are hard feelings about one person being selected for promotion over others.

The dialogue between Mike and Sean suggests that Mike harbors some resentment toward Sean for being selected as manager instead of him. Sean believes that he was promoted, in part, due to his level of commitment to the job and willingness to keep abreast of industry changes that might impact his work. He'd like to believe that Mike has the same level of commitment, but he's not seeing it demonstrated. In truth, Mike has always been a bit of a slacker and a complainer. As his manager, Sean anticipates that he will have to counsel Mike about doing a better job meeting deadlines and achieving goals.

> **• TIP #23 •**
>
> Clarification of new respective roles and responsibilities between you and former coworkers affects all aspects of performance appraisals, including coaching and counseling.

Establish Expectations

The process of preparing to conduct appraisals on former coworkers continues with establishing expectations. While your promotion might not impact the actual duties and responsibilities of your former coworkers, the change in your working relationship can alter the effectiveness of their performance. Therefore, it's important to learn what your former coworkers expect of you as their manager, as well as making known your expectations of them.

Picture this scenario: Jean is promoted to be the manager of one of her coworkers and close friends, Cheryl, who also wanted the job. Jean and Cheryl both agreed before applying that each of them would be supportive of the other if selected. When Cheryl learns that Jean is chosen, she extends enthusiastic congratulations and arranges to take Jean out to dinner to celebrate. Everything is going well until dessert—that's when

Cheryl starts talking about how she sees their new working relationship. As Jean listens, she realizes that Cheryl is presenting her with a list of expectations. Of course, that's not how she puts it, but being a natural list maker, it's how Jean hears Cheryl's rhetoric. She finds herself separating those expectations that sound reasonable from those she deems questionable.

Reasonable Employee Expectations

Here are some of the expectations that Jean finds reasonable:

- Cheryl and Jean will remain friends, although, admittedly, it probably won't be the way it was. For example, it's unlikely they'll be going to lunch or hanging out after work with others from the department as often as they once did.
- Jean will let Cheryl continue to work independently; after all, Cheryl knows her job well and never required close supervision.
- Jean will support Cheryl's desire to apply for tuition reimbursement so she can pursue plans to acquire a business degree.
- Cheryl assures Jean that she'll keep her up to speed on what's going on at the staff level.

Questionable Employee Expectations

Here are some of the thoughts Cheryl expressed that Jean finds questionable:

- Giving Cheryl first crack at overtime assignments.
- Occasionally looking the other way when Cheryl needs extra paid time off or returns late from lunch.
- Approving Cheryl's request to attend an offsite training seminar requiring travel and lodging when a similar course is offered within commuting distance.
- Working from home on occasion, even though the company doesn't have a formal "remote employee" program.

- Recommending Cheryl as a leader in the mentor program, even though she fails to meet all the required criteria.
- Putting Cheryl in charge of the rest of the staff when Jean is out of the office.

Jean agrees that the working relationship will invariably change between them, but she's uncomfortable with some of what she's hearing. Cheryl seems to be telling her how it's going to be, putting herself in charge. Jean doesn't want to pull rank, but it's evident that she needs to address what Cheryl has said in order to move forward with their new working relationship in a productive way: "Cheryl, I agree that aspects of our working relationship will, unavoidably, need to change. I anticipate that there are going to be awkward moments when you might want something from me that I can't deliver on. For example, I can't make a blanket promise that you may take time off whenever you want, or that you may attend conferences in San Francisco when the same program is being offered here, in New York. People know that we're friends, and I'm sure you don't want anyone accusing me of granting—or you of receiving—preferential treatment. That wouldn't bode well for either one of us. I can, however, assure you that I will be fair and objective in my observations and decisions. In exchange, I expect you to feel free to come to me at any time with questions, comments, suggestions, and concerns."

• TIP #24 •

While your promotion might not impact the actual duties and responsibilities of your former coworkers, the change in your working relationship can alter their performance. Therefore, it's important to learn what your former coworkers expect of you as their manager, as well as to make known your expectations of them.

Guidelines for Conducting Appraisals on Former Coworkers

In addition to clarifying respective roles and establishing expectations, you can use these guidelines to help remain focused when preparing to conduct appraisals on former coworkers:

• *Practice introspection.* Take a good look at the influence that you could have on a former coworker's performance, both positively and negatively. Further determine whether that influence skews your ability to evaluate the employee's work objectively.

• *Compare past and current relationships with coworkers.* Before evaluating the work of former coworkers from the perspective of "the boss," step back and assess how you used to relate to their work when you were colleagues. This comparative perspective can help you maintain focus and objectivity as you prepare to conduct performance appraisals through a manager's eye.

• *Address issues, not personalities.* Suppose you have two direct reports, both of whom regularly come in late. One, a friend, has childcare issues with which you are familiar because you used to talk to one another about it as coworkers. The other is also a former coworker but not someone you got along with. He does his work well enough but comes across as standoffish and unfriendly. Regardless of their respective personalities, the issue for both is the same: punctuality, and that's what needs to be addressed, fairly and consistently.

• *Focus on work-related matters.* Coworkers naturally learn a lot about one another's personal lives, including political views, favorite sports teams, religious beliefs, and the like, by virtue of working side-by-side on a daily basis. When you become a manager and are responsible for evaluating the work of your former coworkers, it's impossible to pretend that you no longer know these things. However, how a person thinks when it comes to non-work-related issues should have no bearing whatsoever on his or her performance evaluations.

• *Treat former coworkers the same as other employees.* Sometimes this means ignoring requests for favoritism. Former coworkers are notorious for asking for special treatment when it comes to performance reviews. They may come to you with lines such as "You remember how it was, don't you? You know there's no way I could have met that deadline with all the other work I have to do!" Together, you can look into their workload, but if meeting a certain deadline is a reasonable aspect of their job, then you can't look the other way.

• *Draw from the experiences of other first-time managers.* It sometimes helps to talk with other new managers who also have had to evaluate the performance of former coworkers. Ask them: *What was the most difficult issue you had to confront? How did you overcome it? In hindsight, what, if anything, would you now do differently?* Answers to questions such as these can fortify you, making the process more palatable and productive.

• *Proceed with confidence.* First-time managers who have to evaluate the work of former coworkers often feel uneasy and self-conscious, especially when it comes to poor performers. In order to be taken seriously and be perceived as a manager worthy of respect, you have to establish your authority and credibility; that includes identifying and critiquing areas requiring improvement.

• *Reiterate your goal.* Regularly remind yourself that the primary objective of a performance appraisal is to ensure the maximum utilization of every employee's skills, knowledge, and interests.

• TIP #25 •

Addressing issues and not personalities, focusing on work-related matters, and treating former coworkers the same as other employees can help you remain focused as you prepare to conduct appraisals on former coworkers.

Forms and Ratings

Performance-appraisal forms come in numerous formats, ranging from all essays to total reliance on numerical or descriptive ratings. Some try to cover too much; others err on the side of extreme brevity. Room for employee input varies from nothing to space equal to that of the appraiser. The ideal form combines descriptive terms requiring supporting comments with ample space for employees to comment on their manager's evaluation.

It behooves you to be aware of the overall purpose and multiple uses of evaluation forms, recognize various rating terminology, and know some of the factors that are typically evaluated.

> **• TIP #26 •**
>
> The ideal performance-appraisal form combines descriptive terms requiring supporting comments with providing ample space for employees to comment on their manager's evaluation.

How Forms Are Used and Misused

The primary purpose of a performance-appraisal form is to facilitate the face-to-face meeting between appraising managers and the employees being reviewed. As such, forms can serve as the foundation for face-to-face meetings between you and your employees, and provide invaluable support to the performance appraisal process.

Ways in Which Appraisal Forms Are Effectively Used

Performance appraisal forms are maximally effective when they are used to highlight employees' performance from the last review, or date of hire, to the present, in relation to the requirements and responsibilities as identified in the job description. Specifically, they serve to summarize strengths and areas requiring improvement in relation to the employees' tasks and responsibilities. Remember the first golden rule of performance appraisals: Nothing said during a performance appraisal meeting should ever come as a surprise to an employee (Chapter 4). This rule pertains both to what's said during the performance appraisal meeting and what's written on the form. You should be coaching (Chapter 2) and counseling (Chapter 3) throughout the year, so that what appears on the appraisal form serves as a recap.

Performance appraisal forms can also be used to:

- Support a career-development plan, enabling the employee to build on his or her strengths
- Develop an action plan, including methods and a timetable for improvement
- Establish job-specific goals to be met by the time of the next formal performance appraisal
- Make decisions about promotions, transfers, demotions, terminations, and salary increases, consistent with company policy
- Help human resources ensure relevance between appraisal conclusions and recommendations about promotions, transfers, demotions, terminations, and salary increases, as appropriate
- Enhance coaching and counseling conducted throughout the appraisal period

- Document the need for training
- Allow employees the opportunity to openly express their views about your assessment

Well-designed forms can help employers achieve these objectives, while poorly designed or misused forms can render the system virtually useless. For this reason, adopting another organization's form is not recommended, no matter how similar the other workplace may be in composition, size, or goals. Your form should reflect your organization's unique work environment.

• TIP #27 •

Performance-appraisal forms are maximally effective when they are used to highlight an employee's performance from the last review, or date of hire, to the present, in relation to the requirements and responsibilities as identified in the job description.

Ways In Which Appraisal Forms Are Misused

One of the most common misuses of performance-appraisal forms is for managers to complete and submit them to HR without first discussing the contents with the employee. This translates into a lost opportunity for the employee to discuss the various categories being evaluated or to review means for improving performance. It also precludes the opportunity for managers and employees to set performance objectives together for the next review period.

Here are some additional common misuses of performance-appraisal forms:

• *Meeting with employees to discuss their performance prior to completing the form.* The manager may use the blank form as a guide for the meeting, reviewing the various categories and commenting verbally on the employee's performance in each, but without anything written down. The employee has no way of knowing exactly what, if anything, the manager will record and whether the employee may have said anything to influence what's ultimately written.

• *Completing the form and submitting it to the employee for review, comment, and signature.* This negates any face-to-face discussion, a vital part of the appraisal process. Face-to-face interaction between you and the employee is essential for maintaining a positive working relationship, planning objectives for the next review period, and encouraging career development.

• *Changing comments on the form after meeting face-to-face with the employee.* These changes are often negative and typically occur when then employee says something during the interview that makes the appraiser think she was too generous with the original rating. Sometimes, however, managers are convinced by employees that they were originally too harsh, and upgrade the ratings accordingly.

• *Relying too heavily on numerical ratings.* This commonly occurs because numerical ratings may strike you as easy to use; however, it's this perceived ease of use that renders them ineffective when they stand alone, providing an inadequate portrayal of employee performance. If your organization's form uses numerical ratings, it should also provide ample space for supportive statements.

Rating Terminology

There is a limitless range of rating terminology available for use on performance-appraisal forms. Not only is there an assortment of language from which to choose, but there are also multiple groups of terms from which organizations can typically select. Each grouping has advantages and disadvantages.

Five Grouping Terms

Here are some examples of five grouping terms:

• *Far exceeds* the requirements of the job; *exceeds* the requirements of the job; *meets* the requirements of the job; *occa-*

sionally meets the requirements of the job; *fails to meet* the requirements of the job

- *Always meets* the requirements of the job; *consistently meets* the requirements of the job; *often* meets the requirements of the job; *sometimes meets* the requirements of the job; *rarely meets* the requirements of the job

- *Invariably meets* the requirements of the job; *regularly meets* the requirements of the job; *usually meets* the requirements of the job; *occasionally meets* the requirements of the job; *never meets* the requirements of the job

Five grouping terms are the most popular. Managers report that they can make a more accurate selection from among five statements. On the other hand, with five choices comes the inevitable middle-of-the-road term, which, regardless of the actual word used, translates into "average" or "satisfactory." If you're uneasy about doling out criticism or praise, it's an easy option. To keep from falling into this trap, some organizations design their five-term groupings so that the order is switched around for each category being rated. This has roughly the effect of a speed bump in that the appraiser has to slow down and read each statement to ensure that the right one is being checked off. Ideally, upon reading the descriptions accompanying each rating, the appraiser will put some thought into selecting the one that best reflects the employee's work, backing it up with specific examples.

Four Grouping Terms

Consider these examples of popular four grouping terms:

- *Superior* performance; *commendable* performance; *acceptable* performance; *unacceptable* performance

- *Extraordinary* work; *excellent* work; *good* work; *poor* work

- *Outstanding ability* to meet job expectations; *good ability* to meet job expectations; *fair ability* to meet job expectations; *poor ability* to meet job expectations

Four grouping terms are desirable in that they do not suffer from that middle rating syndrome associated with five grouping terms. However, having four choices can compel appraisers to select from what is perceived as either the positive or negative side.

Three Grouping Terms

Some employers opt for three grouping terms, believing that it makes your job easier:

- *Above*-average performance; *average* performance; *below*-average performance
- *Exceeds* expectations; *meets* expectations; *fails to meet* expectations
- *Exceptional* work; *Acceptable* work; *unacceptable* work

Three grouping terms are, by their very nature, limiting. They also present the same dilemma as five grouping terms in that there is a middle "average" choice. On the other hand, some managers say that they like three choices because they find it easier to select from among three, broad terms.

The most effective way to avoid problems associated with each of these methods is to require supporting statements and examples to accompany each rating. That way, regardless of whether a five-, four-, or three-term rating is chosen, there is a rationale for your selection.

Definitions of Terms

Providing definitions directly on the form of what each term means will help you gauge that which is the most appropriate term to select. For example, let's consider a five-term rating consisting of "outstanding," "very good," "good," "improvement needed," and "unsatisfactory." Accompanying definitions could read as follows:

- *Outstanding*: Consistently performs at an exceptional level.

- *Very Good:* Frequently performs at a high level.
- *Good:* Regularly performs in a competent manner.
- *Improvement Needed.* Demonstrates need for performance and/or skills development.
- *Unsatisfactory.* Performance results are unacceptable.

• TIP #28 •

The most effective way to avoid problems associated with five-, four-, or three-term ratings is to require supporting statements and examples to accompany each rating.

Factors to Be Evaluated

Ratings and accompanying definitions help guide managers as they review the factors to be evaluated. Since most organizations have a maximum of two performance-appraisal forms (one for everyone, or one for exempt and another for nonexempt employees), these factors are, of necessity, generic in nature. As such, they should be defined in clear and concise terms so that everyone interprets them the same way.

Here are some of the factors and accompanying definitions that typically appear on performance-appraisal forms:

- *Adherence to Policies and Procedures:* The extent to which an employee follows organizational and departmental policies and procedures.
- *Attendance:* The extent to which an employee meets the time requirements of his or her regularly scheduled workweek.
- *Creativity.* The extent to which an employee develops different and improved approaches to perform tasks.
- *Independence:* The extent to which an employee is able to work with little or no supervision.

- *Interpersonal Relationships:* The extent to which an employee demonstrates an ability and willingness to cooperate and work effectively with others.
- *Initiative.* The extent to which an employee seeks out new assignments and takes on additional responsibilities.
- *Job Knowledge.* The extent to which an employee understands what's necessary to perform the duties and responsibilities of the job effectively.
- *Judgment.* The extent to which an employee demonstrates and exercises effective decision-making skills.
- *Productivity.* The extent to which an employee produces a specified volume of work in a given period of time.
- *Quality of Work.* The extent to which an employee's work is accurate, thorough, and neat.
- *Reliability.* The extent to which an employee can be counted on to complete a given task in an accurate and timely manner.

• TIP #29 •

The factors appearing on a performance-appraisal form are usually generic in nature. As such, they should be defined in clear and concise terms so that everyone interprets them the same way.

Here's a scenario illustrating the use of rating terminology and factors to be evaluated, as they appear on an appraisal form:

Laura is preparing to conduct a performance appraisal on her administrative assistant, Jed. Her company uses the five-term rating system described earlier: *Outstanding*: consistently performs at an exceptional level; *Very Good:* frequently performs at a high level; *Good:* regularly performs in a competent manner; *Improvement Needed:* demonstrates need for performance and/or skills development; *Unsatisfactory:* performance results are unacceptable.

Here's how Laura rates Jed on three of the eleven general factors on the form: initiative, job knowledge, and adherence to policies and procedures (The X's represents specific examples that Laura will later provide to support her rating for each factor.)

- *Factor:* Initiative
  Rating: Outstanding
  Rationale: Jed constantly takes it upon himself to come up with useful suggestions to help the department resolve problems with our information system. For example, XXXXXXXXXXXXXXX. In addition, Jed frequently seeks out new assignments, such as XXXXXXXXXXXXXX.
- *Factor: Job Knowledge*
  Rating: Outstanding
  Rationale: There's no question that Jed knows what's necessary in order to perform his job effectively. The extent of his proficiency prevents the necessity of redoing any assignments, allowing him more time to devote to developing solutions to departmental problems. (See comments accompanying "initiative.") Specifically, XXX XXXXXXXXXXXX.
- *Factor: Adherence to Policies and Procedures*
  Rating: Improvement Needed
  Rationale: On a number of occasions, Jed has indicated that he has no qualms about bending the rules now and then in order to get his job done as efficiently as possible. Despite several talks with him about this (see attached coaching notes), Jed continues to disregard policies and procedures when they "get in his way." Here are two specific examples: (1) XXXXXXXXXXXXXXX. (2) XXXXXXX XXXXXXXX.

In this scenario, the definition of the ratings and accompanying explanation of each factor enable Laura to rate Jed's performance accurately and objectively. In Chapter 8, we'll learn more about what she might actually write.

• 8 •

Writing Guidelines

Good managers don't always write good performance appraisals. Here's a review prepared by Rob, an intelligent, hardworking, well-respected manager. He rated his review as being ". . . very good: succinct and to the point."

Do you agree with his assessment?

Job Title: Marketing Assistant

Factor: Quality of Work	*Comment:* Excellent
Factor: Productivity	*Comment:* Great job last Friday!
Factor: Job Knowledge	*Comment:* Knows his stuff
Factor: Reliability	*Comment:* Very good with paperwork
Factor: Attendance	*Comment:* Fine
Factor: Independence	*Comment:* Very good
Factor: Creativity	*Comment:* Could come up with more ideas
Factor: Decision making	*Comment:* Good
Factor: Cooperation	*Comment:* Needs to work on it

Overall rating: Mostly very good

The brevity of his words, poor language selection, and reference to a single, recent event all reflect Rob's lack of understanding as to the skills necessary to write an effective performance evaluation. Rob is also guilty of a problem that many managers share, especially those who are new to the job; that is, how to do justice to an employee by summarizing a year's worth of job performance on a single sheet of paper. To accomplish this seemingly daunting task, they struggle to be concise to such an extent that the content is skimpy and filled with meaningless generalities.

Writing performance appraisals that are substantive, yet contained in terms of length, is actually a manageable task. The process begins with identifying and selecting objective language, then becoming familiar with basic writing dos and don'ts, and finally adhering to an easy-to-follow, seven-step writing format.

Selecting Objective Language

Objective language is impartial and likely to be interpreted similarly by most people. On the other hand, subjective language reflects one's personal opinion, may be subject to interpretation, and fails to communicate relevant, concrete information. The bottom line: All language selected for written performance appraisals should be objective.

Effective Terminology

Objective terminology is most effective when it has a direct correlation with the duties and tasks for which employees are responsible; that is, performance should be measured in relation to pre-existing standards, as identified in job descriptions (Chapter 5). All supporting examples should also be objective, specific, and quantified, whenever possible. For example: "Victor exceeded his sales goals by 15 percent three months in a row" is objective, specific, and quantified.

Here are thirty-five positive and negative evaluative phrases commonly used in written performance appraisals. Remember to provide supportive examples. Note the use of action verbs at the start of each phrase:

- *Achieves* cost-effective results
- *Applies* sound analytical skills
- *Attains* results but often sacrifices accuracy
- *Avoids* breakdowns in production
- *Communicates* decisions with confidence
- *Creates* new approaches to problem-solving
- *Demonstrates* a strong ability to resolve conflicts
- *Devotes* additional time to the job, as needed
- *Directs* peers effectively in team projects
- *Disagrees* respectfully
- *Displays* complete knowledge of technical aspects of the job
- *Enforces* departmental rules
- *Excels* in maintaining detailed accounts
- *Exhibits* erratic patterns of punctuality and attendance
- *Fails* to fulfill job expectations
- *Falls short* when it comes to meeting deadlines
- *Focuses* on only one task at a time
- *Forgets* to submit quarterly budget for review
- *Generates* suggestions and new ideas
- *Grasps* new concepts quickly
- *Inspires* confidence
- *Improperly monitors* the release of proprietary information
- *Keeps* accurate records
- *Lacks* initiative to take on additional responsibilities
- *Maintains* a high level of cost-control practices
- *Makes* an exceptionally high number of errors
- *Manages* multiple tasks simultaneously
- *Maximizes* use of her time
- *Possesses* a strong understanding of departmental goals
- *Repeatedly* asks the same questions
- *Responds* expeditiously to requests for additional information

- *Sets* excessively high standards
- *Works* well with colleagues and members of senior management

Objective Evaluations of Varying Levels of Performance

Objective language can be used to evaluate outstanding, average, and marginal employees. Here are three examples of objective comments for the category "Job Knowledge":

1. *Outstanding Employee:* Carolyn demonstrates an in-depth understanding of both the practical and technical knowledge needed to perform her job, far exceeding that which is required. She is also willing to impart that knowledge to coworkers who are having difficulty understanding certain aspects of their jobs. (Note: Specific examples would elaborate on instances in which Carolyn has helped coworkers.)

2. *Average Employee:* Clarke demonstrates a sound understanding of the practical knowledge required for his job but resists help with certain technical aspects that he's not as well versed in. This, in turn, occasionally prevents him from completing his work in a timely fashion. (Note: Specific examples would elaborate on instances in which Clarke's diminished technical knowledge has prevented him from completing his work on time.)

3. *Marginal Employee:* Lana possesses a marginally acceptable level of knowledge with which to perform her job, with her technical knowledge slightly outweighing her practical knowledge. This is not due to a lack of effort on her part; she simply does not seem to grasp the fundamentals required to perform her work. This has resulted in other employees having to perform some of her tasks, which has produced a growing morale problem. (Note: Specific examples would elaborate on examples of Lana's effort to become more knowledgeable about her job, as well as to describe specific instances in which Lana's limited job knowledge has resulted in other employees having to do her work in addition to their own.)

> **• TIP #30 •**
>
> Language selected for written performance appraisals should be objective. Objective language is impartial and likely to be interpreted similarly by most people. Conversely, subjective language reflects one's personal opinion, may be subject to interpretation, and fails to communicate relevant, concrete information.

Writing Dos and Don'ts

Conveying a certain written tone and using a particular writing style will set the stage for a maximally productive face-to-face meeting. Simply stated, your tone should be direct, factual, and positive; your style moderate to formal, with limited jargon and clichés.

Here are some guidelines to help first-time managers write effective performance reviews:

Writing Dos

1. *Do* begin planning the written performance appraisal approximately one month prior to the due date, jotting down thoughts as they occur to you.
2. *Do* write the review, and then put it away for a few days. Then, return to it, and read it from multiple perspectives, including your own, that of the employee, and that of human resources.
3. *Do* use the employee's job description as the foundation for your written review, striving to link each comment with specific job duties and responsibilities.
4. *Do* support each rating with examples and facts.
5. *Do* be prepared to discuss supporting examples.
6. *Do* try to present a balanced picture of strengths and areas requiring improvement.
7. *Do* look at an employee's entire performance record since his last review, date of hire, or date of most recent job change—whichever is applicable.

8. *Do* consider the employee's self evaluation, as well as evaluations solicited from others, such as colleagues and clients.

9. *Do* ensure that the written review clearly conveys what is expected of the employee, as well as what is acceptable and what is not.

10. *Do* strive for consistency between your evaluation and any corresponding recommendations, including salary increases, if called for.

11. *Do* evaluate performance, and not personality.

12. *Do* be honest.

Writing Don'ts

1. *Don't* allow how well an employee performs in certain categories to influence your ratings in other categories. For example, an employee's job knowledge may be outstanding, but it doesn't make up for the fact that he is unreliable.

2. *Don't* make up strengths or areas requiring improvement that don't exist, for the sake of creating a balanced picture.

3. *Don't* be influenced by first impressions or past performance to the extent that you overlook legitimate performance-related issues.

4. *Don't* use the same words to evaluate all employees.

5. *Don't* use absolutes, such as "always" and "never."

6. *Don't* downplay poor performance just because you're concerned about hurting an employee's feelings or worried that an employee will no longer like you after reading her review.

7. *Don't* introduce anything new. Remember: Nothing that's said or written during the performance appraisal process should come as a surprise to an employee.

8. *Don't* play it safe by selecting the middle evaluation term for all performance factors.

9. *Don't* be overly influenced by recent job performance—whether positive or negative; remember that you are evaluating performance over the entire review period.

10. *Don't* be tempted to dole out higher ratings to those whose views or characteristics are similar to your own.

11. *Don't* make excuses for performance flaws because of personal issues.

12. *Don't* say anything that cannot be supported by facts.

> ### • TIP #31 •
>
> Conveying a certain written tone and using a particular writing style will set the stage for a maximally productive face-to-face meeting. Simply stated, your tone should be direct, factual, and positive; your style moderate to formal, with limited jargon and clichés.

A Seven-Step Writing Format

The following seven-step format for written performance appraisals is simple, yet highly effective when it comes to ensuring consistency and uniformity: two factors that are critical to ensuring that employees know they are being evaluated according to the same standards as everyone else. The approach is applicable to virtually every workplace, is appropriate for all employee classifications, and works with any type of appraisal form, regardless of the categories included. Optimum results will be achieved if self-evaluations by employees are also factored in.

> ### • TIP #32 •
>
> The success of any performance-appraisal program is rooted in consistency and uniformity; that is, all managers following the same format so employees know they are being evaluated according to the same standards as everyone else.

Step 1: Overview

Provide a two- to three-sentence summary of the employee's performance since her last review or date of hire. Avoid referencing specific incidences. Here's an example:

Since the date of her last annual review, Veronica has continued to exhibit an in-depth understanding of her job. She consistently performs her responsibilities in an exemplary fashion, serving as a role model for new hires.

Step 2: Strengths

Identify employee strengths, supported by specific examples. Try to highlight examples that reflect a variety of assignments performed under varying circumstances throughout the year. Also try to reflect different strengths, especially those reflecting growth and development since the time of hire or the last review.

Step 3: Areas Requiring Improvement

Identify areas in which the employee requires improvement, supported by specific examples. Be careful not to preface any statements with terminology like "I think . . ." or "In my opinion. . . ." Areas requiring improvement should be job-specific, as well as tangible or quantitative.

Step 4: Meeting Previously Agreed-Upon Goals

Review the employee's success in meeting goals that were mutually agreed-upon at the time of the last review or time of hire. Cite the goal, then specify exactly what the employee did or did not do toward meeting that goal. Avoid generalizations, such as "Jen needs to keep working hard so she can meet the goals she set last year."

Step 5: Setting New Goals

Identify mutually agreed-upon goals for the employee to accomplish by the date of his next appraisal. Goals should be clear, measurable, time-tied, and focus on results. For example, "Launch four new testing programs in the coming fiscal year" meets the criteria of being clear, measurable, and time-tied, and it also focuses on results.

Develop a timeline with interim meetings set to review

progress, and identify any problems encountered by the employee as she strives to meet these goals. New goals may also include a carry-over of goals from the last meeting. Revisit them as needed, ensuring that they are achievable and desirable from the employee's perspective.

While goals should be mutually agreed-upon, managers play a greater role in specifying goals for work that is primarily *prefigured*; that is, routine, repetitive tasks. Managers generally solicit goals from the employee for work that is primarily *configured*; that is, nonroutine tasks.

Step 6: Career Development

Encourage employees to discuss career goals and aspirations. Together, you can identify how the employee will achieve personal and professional development; for example, through seminars, training, and schooling. These goals should linked, as closely as possible, with organizational goals.

Step 7: Employee Feedback

Solicit employee signatures and written comments on the performance-appraisal form. The employee's signature signifies understanding of the contents, and not necessarily agreement. Any comments, while unlikely to result in a changed evaluation, can serve to enhance future employer-employee relations.

• TIP #33 •

Following a seven-step format for written reviews ensures consistency and uniformity. The format consists of: providing an overview; identifying employee strengths; identifying areas requiring improvement; reviewing success in meeting previously agreed-upon goals; setting new goals; identifying career-development plans; and soliciting employee feedback.

• 9 •

How to Begin

Everything you've read thus far leads to the face-to-face meeting between you and your employees. As with job applicants, for whom the first few minutes set the tone for the rest of the interview, so, too, does the beginning of a performance appraisal meeting determine the course that the rest of the meeting is likely to take. Specifically, you need to be attuned to the environment in which the meeting takes place and focus on putting the employee at ease. But first, ask yourself some important questions.

> ### • TIP #34 •
> What takes place at the beginning of a performance appraisal meeting sets the tone for the rest of the meeting.

Questions to Ask Yourself

While sitting in his office waiting for Jill to arrive for her annual performance review, Russell runs through a mental list to ensure that he's completely prepared:

- Russell has factored in notes from coaching and counseling sessions throughout the year.

75

- Jill will not be hearing about anything performance-related for the first time.
- Jill's job description served as the framework for the evaluation.
- Russell has input from several sources according to the company's 360-degree evaluation guidelines.
- Jill has prepared a self-appraisal.
- All language is in full compliance with employment legislation (Appendix B).
- Every rating is supported with examples.
- Every statement is objective.
- Russell completed the evaluation form according to appraisal-writing guidelines.

Russell notes that he's counted nine items: Something is missing. He knows there's one more thing he needs to do just before meeting with Jill, but what? Ah, yes: There are some questions he's supposed to ask himself to maximally ensure that Jill receives a fair and objective evaluation. Russell's self-examination soliloquy goes something like this:

- Am I confident that the employee's skills and interests are properly aligned with the job?
- Is there enough of a match between the employee and myself with regard to important intangible factors, such as management style or personality, to ensure a productive working relationship?
- Does the employee have a clear understanding of the job duties and scope of responsibilities?
- Have I worked with the employee long enough (at least three months) to be able to evaluate her performance effectively?
- Have I objectively measured the employee's work record against the requirements of the job?

- Have I evaluated the employee's entire performance and not just identified isolated positive or negative incidences?

- Do I have some ideas as to how improvements can best be accomplished?

- Have I determined what assistance I'm prepared to provide toward improvement?

- Has the employee been provided with sufficient instructions and work tools?

- Have I encouraged the employee to ask questions or seek clarification regarding her work assignments?

- Have I anticipated the feelings and possible reactions of the employee?

- Have I explored my own feelings and ensured that I am approaching the meeting with a mind that is open and free of bias?

- Am I prepared to listen to what the employee has to say, without feeling defensive?

- Have I been available and supportive during instances when the employee has had an especially difficult assignment or challenging deadline to meet?

If the answer to any of these questions is no, then an employee's unsatisfactory performance might have nothing to do with ability; instead, it could be the product of your failure to:

- Set mutually agreed-upon meaningful objectives
- Accurately measure accomplishments against agreed-upon objectives
- Examine personal attitudes that could interfere with an objective measurement of performance

This last statement may be the most difficult to accept: After all, no one wants to think that they are anything other than impartial and nonjudgmental. Yet, posing this and the other questions just prior to the appraisal meeting could make the difference between a productive and nonproductive session.

> **• TIP #35 •**
>
> Ask yourself some key questions just prior to conducting face-to-face performance-appraisal meetings to maximally ensure that employees receive fair and objective evaluations.

Create a Suitable Environment

Meeting in a suitable environment will maximize the effectiveness of any appraisal session, especially awkward ones, such as those in which areas requiring improvement are likely to be emphasized. There are four essential ingredients to creating a suitable environment: privacy, a distraction-free location, comfort, and allowing adequate time.

Privacy

Can you imagine receiving your performance appraisal while walking en route to a meeting? How about in the back of a cab? Would hearing your manager discussing areas in which you need to improve, over lunch within earshot of coworkers, be better? How about while riding in an elevator? Or perhaps you'd prefer to run into your manager at the mall where, while shopping, she evaluates your success in meeting goals set during your last review?

These are actual examples of some of the most unconventional, and inappropriate, settings in which managers have conducted performance appraisals. If I didn't know that these and several other equally bizarre occurrences were true, I would not feel compelled to mention the obvious: Performance-appraisal meetings should be conducted in private. Employees must believe that what they're saying is confidential and cannot be overheard by others. This is particularly important when sensitive matters are being discussed, such as repeated and unresolved performance problems.

Some appraising managers believe a neutral location, such as a conference room, is preferable to their office or the employee's workspace, negating any possibility that one or the other has a "home court advantage." That's fine, as long as the location is private, private, private.

Minimum Number of Distractions

Put yourself in this employee's place: She arrived at the appointed time for her annual performance review, entered her manager's office, and sat down. He greeted her, ceremoniously rose from his chair, came around his desk, and closed the door. He then began talking about her work. Within minutes, there was a knock on his door: "I'm sorry to bother you," said his secretary, "but Mr. Reynolds is here and just needs a minute of your time." Her manager didn't hesitate: "Sure, tell him to come in." Their conversation indeed lasted only a few minutes, and the meeting between my friend and her manager continued. But then the phone rang, and he answered it. This was followed by another knock on the door. The worst offense, according to my friend, was when she asked him a question and he didn't initially reply; when he finally did, he started with "Sorry, I was just thinking about all the work I have to do!"

How inspired would you be to continue working for this manager?

Comfort

You can be assured of a more productive meeting if employees are physically comfortable and feel at ease. Indeed, it's your behavior and general approach to the meeting that effectively determines the comfort level of the employee. If you come across as friendly, appear genuinely interested in what the employee has to say, and have made an effort to ensure privacy and prevent interruptions, then the physical trappings are not going to matter all that much.

Sufficient Time for the Interview

In determining how much time to set aside for the appraisal meeting, begin by factoring in the time needed before the meeting to review relevant paperwork. This includes your completed form; reviews done by others; the employee's self-evaluation; coaching and counseling documentation; and information concerning previous goals. Next, consider time during the meeting to discuss past performance, previous and future goals, and the employee's career development. Finally, allow time after the meeting to reflect on what took place as well as to finalize any paperwork.

Considering all that must be done, just how much time should be set aside for each appraisal meeting? In part, the answer rests with the complexity of the employee's job, the scope of the ratings, and the employee's likely reaction. Generally speaking, set aside a total of 90 minutes, with 60 minutes for the face-to-face meeting. That leaves approximately 30 minutes to be divided between the pre- and post-meeting activities.

Scheduling Guidelines

To help maximize the time set aside for meeting applicants, consider these scheduling guidelines:

• Try to conduct appraisal meetings during that part of the day when you're most alert. If you tend to slow down in mid afternoon, it would be best to schedule meetings during the morning hours. Also try to consider the employee's schedule, both in terms of peak hours and workflow.

• Some organizations schedule all performance reviews at the same time of the year, while others use the individual employee's "anniversary" date of hire. If you work for a company that requires its managers to submit all appraisals on the same date, you could find yourself with a number of meetings scheduled back-to-back. If that happens to you, try to take a 30-minute break between meetings. This will allow you to make the transition from one employee to the other as well as granting greater control of your appraisal schedule.

• Try not to conduct more than three meetings in one day. For example, 9:00 A.M. to 10:30 A.M.; 11:00 A.M. to 12:30 P.M.; and 2:00 P.M. to 3:30 P.M. Obviously, this may not always be possible if you're on a same-date review system and are in charge of numerous employees. However, if you can schedule your meetings in between other work, you'll find that your attention level during the meetings and the quality of your other work are likely to improve.

• TIP #36 •

There are four essential ingredients to creating a suitable environment: privacy, a distraction-free location, comfort, and adequate time.

Put Employees at Ease

Regardless of how well you know your employees, don't overlook the importance of devoting a few moments at the beginning of the meeting to ensure that they feel at ease.

Icebreakers

Putting employees at ease is best accomplished with icebreakers; that is, comments and questions that have no direct bearing on the purpose of the meeting. Their sole function is to maximize the employee's comfort level before the actual meeting begins. *For example:*

• I'm glad you made it in this morning. I shoveled for hours after last night's snow, just so I could dig out my car!
• Did you get caught in that traffic jam on the parkway? I never did figure out what caused it—all of a sudden, cars just started moving!

- It's nice to see the sun shining for a change; five consecutive rainy days are enough for me!
- Did you have a smooth commute this morning?

Notice that all of these icebreakers have to do with the same two benign topics: weather and travel. Remember: Your objective is to put the employee at ease. As such, avoid controversial or personal subjects; that is, any topic that could trigger a strong reaction on the part of the employee and, in turn, aversely impact the appraisal meeting.

Just how much time should be spent on icebreakers depends on how comfortable the employee appears to be. In most instances, fifteen to thirty seconds is sufficient. Rarely should this stage of the interview continue for more than a minute or so. Employees who still appear to be uneasy after this amount of time will probably not respond to additional small talk. The best thing to do in such an instance is to get started.

Try to link the icebreakers with your opening remarks, thereby eliminating the awkward silence that can easily occur. For example, "Why don't we get started; perhaps it will help take your mind off the fact that you got soaked coming over here!"

Opening Remarks

While both you and the employee obviously know why you're meeting, your opening remarks set the pace for what follows and alert the employee as to what he can expect over the next hour or so. Here are two examples of opening remarks, reflecting two distinct styles:

Example #1: "Hi, Mark; have a seat. I'm glad you're here; I'm looking forward to talking with you about your performance over the past year. We'll also look at some of your goals for the upcoming year. This is *your* review, Mark; I'm looking forward to us having a dialogue that includes your comments and questions."

The manager in this example has a casual, laid-back style, setting the stage for an informal meeting. The employee knows from the outset that he can expect two-way communication.

Example #2: "Good morning, Mark. Please, come in and have a seat. I trust you've completed your self-evaluation, as requested. I have my review of your work over the past year, which I'll be comparing with your self-assessment. In keeping with the company's 360-degree appraisal policy, I also have input from three of your colleagues and two clients with whom you regularly work. We'll review their feedback together. Next, we'll discuss how successful you've been in meeting the objectives we agreed to the last time we met, as well as new performance objectives. After that, we'll talk about your career goals and how they fit in with organizational goals. If it's all right with you, to keep from disrupting the flow, I'm going to suggest that you refrain from asking questions or making comments until we're near the end."

This manager is far more reserved and formal, suggesting a more structured approach to the meeting. The employee clearly understands that any discussion will be held to a minimum, and only when the manager's "presentation" is complete.

• TIP #37 •

Regardless of how well you know your employees, be sure to devote time at the beginning of the meeting to ensure that they feel at ease.

•10•

What to Discuss

Many first-time managers erroneously assume that performance assessments are all about how well employees have been
performing their jobs to date. While no one will dispute the
fact that past performance is an important part of the process,
there's much more to the face-to-face meeting than reviewing
what the employee has accomplished, or failed to accomplish,
in the past. The most successful performance-appraisal meetings are those that focus on three distinct areas: past performance; previous and future performance objectives; and the
employee's career-development plan.

Adding these last two components into the mix accom-
plishes a great deal:

- They lend balance to the meeting by looking ahead instead of dwelling on the past.
- They validate an employee's efforts, interests, and aspirations.
- They allow for maximum utilization of an organization's
  human resources by identifying common denominators
  between departmental/corporate and personal goals.
- They encourage employees to challenge themselves as
  they strive to meet new goals, thereby increasing levels of
  employee motivation and productivity.

• They allow employees to take more responsibility for, and greater ownership of, future job performance.

If you explore all three of these areas during performance-appraisal meetings, you're likely to observe improved employer-employee relations. Consequently, your superiors will view you as being a more effective manager.

• TIP #38 •

The most successful performance-appraisal meetings are those that focus on three distinct areas: past performance; previous and future performance objectives; and the employee's career-development plan.

Past Performance

Some managers view this segment of the performance-appraisal meeting as an opportunity to dwell on what employees have been doing wrong. This is a mistake. Regardless of how accurate you may be in terms of citing specific examples of past transgressions, would you want to be on the receiving end of a performance review that dwelled on your errors and shortcomings?

In truth, talking about past performance should take no more than the amount of time set aside for discussing goals and career development, regardless of whether the feedback is positive or negative. If appraisal meetings run about an hour, that means approximately twenty minutes spent talking about past performance.

If you are performing your coaching and counseling duties effectively throughout the year (Chapters 2 and 3), then nothing said during the appraisal meeting will come as a surprise to the employee (Chapter 4). The employee will essentially know from the outset how he's going to be evaluated. As such, this portion of the appraisal meeting may best be viewed as a summary, laying the foundation for the rest of the meeting.

Let's illustrate this past point by revisiting two scenarios. The first involves Gwen, a manager, and Vanessa, a customer service representative. As you recall, Gwen was walking by Vanessa's desk (Chapter 2) when she overheard the tail end of Vanessa's side of a phone conversation with a customer. Vanessa was clearly agitated with what she perceived to be the customer's unreasonable demands, and she made her feelings clear to the customer. Gwen coached Vanessa about her approach, and Vanessa offered to rectify the matter. Now, it is several months later, and the two are meeting to discuss Vanessa's annual review. When it comes time to address Vanessa's ability to deal effectively with challenging customer service issues, Gwen says, "While there was that incident when you lost your patience with a customer over the phone, I was impressed with your willingness to try to repair the damage by contacting the customer the next day. In addition, there have not been any additional similar occurrences since that time. That suggests to me that you were able to convert negative behavior into a positive outcome."

The second scenario involves Steve and Angie (Chapter 3). Steve, a manager, has both coached and counseled Angie, a sales associate, concerning her repeated cell phone use for personal calls during working hours. Unfortunately, the matter of Angie's inappropriate phone use remains unresolved as the date of her performance assessment meeting nears. Steve knows that he needs to review the steps taken to date, and then comment on the impact of Angie's failure to amend her behavior on her overall evaluation. During Angie's appraisal meeting, Steve begins, "Angie, as you know, we've talked about the use of your cell phone for personal calls during working hours on a number of occasions. We've discussed how this is a violation of store policy, and you agreed to stop. Unfortunately, you continue to make and receive personal calls while at the register; therefore, I've had to factor your unwillingness to comply with store policy into your overall evaluation. I'd like to hear how you believe you can use this experience to turn this behavior around in the future."

In both examples, the employees know what to expect prior

to the start of the meeting. The managers present the information in the form of summarizing statements and, without dwelling on the negative, move forward.

• TIP #39 •

The portion of the appraisal meeting devoted to past performance may best be viewed as a summary, laying the foundation for the rest of the meeting.

Goals

Many employment interviewers favor questions about job-related goals: "Where do you see yourself in a year?" and "How do you see this job fitting in with your long-term goals?" are two perennial favorites. Questions concerning goal-setting are also germane to performance-appraisal meetings. It's equally important for you to be able to determine how well employees have succeeded in accomplishing past goals, as well as what goals they choose to target for the future.

Previous Goals

As with past performance, if you have done your job effectively throughout the year as a coach and counselor, employees will know in advance of the appraisal meeting how successful they've been in meeting previously set goals. Presumably, you will have sat down together at given intervals to discuss progress and/or challenges encountered. Employees should arrive at the meeting knowing how well they've achieved past goals; what problems, if any, they encountered in their quest to satisfy their goals; and how the manager views their accomplishments.

These results should serve as springboards for setting new performance objectives. For example: "Yul, one of the goals you set for yourself last year was to reduce the number of product-related complaints by 10 percent. As you know, you achieved and exceeded that goal: Product complaints are down by 11.5

percent. You should be extremely pleased with your efforts in this regard; I know I am. What I'd like to ask you now is, 'where do you see yourself going from here?' Do you have additional goals relative to product-related complaints? If so, let's talk about them."

• TIP #40 •

If you've done your job effectively throughout the year as a coach and counselor, employees will know in advance of the appraisal meeting how successful they've been in meeting previously set goals.

Future Goals

Future goals will not necessarily have anything to do with achieving more or working harder. Sometimes, new objectives take the employee in an entirely different direction. Your role throughout this process is that of a facilitator. You can ask questions and make suggestions, but the employee needs to do the bulk of the planning and work.

What Happens If . . .

What happens if there's a conflict between what you see as an appropriate goal for an employee and the employee's objectives? Assuming that the individual's goals are job-related, you need to remember that the most productive employees are those who are motivated, and that motivation is self-generated, driven by a combination of skill and interest. As such, you would do well to hear what the employee has in mind.

What happens if an employee sets his sights lower than you believe he should? You need to set performance expectations at a level that will achieve results in line with the requirements of the job. At the same time, you should constantly encourage employees to do their best. If an employee expresses doubt over being able to accomplish certain goals, talk about specific skills he has demonstrated to date that convince you that he can attain more. Better yet, ask him to identify some of his strengths and how they can work for him in terms of stretching beyond what he's previously done.

What happens if you express thoughts concerning future goals, and the employee says that's not something she believes is her responsibility? First, review the employee's job description, and clarify her tasks. Then, discuss areas of accountability. Both parties need to agree on the employee's function in terms of content and scope before proceeding with a discussion of future goals.

> **• TIP #41 •**
>
> During the future goal-setting stage of an appraisal meeting, you can ask questions and make suggestions, but the employee needs to do the bulk of the planning and work.

Goal-Setting Components

Assuming that both parties agree on areas of responsibility and accountability, you can move on to successful goal-setting via a five-step process:

1. Clearly state the performance objective.
2. Break it down into identifiable and manageable components.
3. Isolate resources needed to accomplish each component.
4. Identify possible barriers.
5. Develop a timeline that will include periodic meetings between you and an employee.

Let's consider the future goal-setting portion of a performance-appraisal meeting between Nicholas, a sales agent, and his manager, Kate. Nicholas has increased revenues in his division by 25 percent. Since his target was 20 percent, no one would argue that Nicholas had succeeded in meeting his previously set performance objectives. Now, it's time for Nicholas to work jointly with Kate to set new performance objectives. At first glance, it might seem logical to suggest that

Nicholas stretch a bit more and strive to increase sales by 30–35 percent. But that's not what he wants. For the next review period, Nicholas would like to set his sights on becoming more creative in his sales approach. This is slightly problematic in that it's not as quantifiable; yet, it's clear that this performance objective will satisfy Nicholas's drive to grow in his job.

Together, Nicholas and Kate should identify a plan for achieving this objective. According to the goal-setting steps, here is Nicholas's plan:

1. *Clearly state the performance objective.* To become more creative in my sales approach by utilizing new techniques.

2. *Break it down into identifiable and manageable components.* To identify and explore various methods for closing deals; to observe other sales approaches first hand; to practice various sales approaches in a simulated environment; and to isolate those sales approaches that are likely to generate increased sales.

3. *Isolate resources needed to accomplish each component.* Reading periodicals and having conversations with other sales agents will help me explore new methods for closing deals; accompanying other agents on sales calls will enable me to observe varying sales approaches first hand; having access to a "practice" environment, with colleagues present, will allow me to experiment with different sales approaches; and talking with my manager about creative sales approaches that will also generate increased sales will help me pinpoint those new approaches that are likely to lead to the achievement of my goal.

4. *Identify possible barriers.* Lack of willingness or availability of other sales agents who can demonstrate different sales approaches; lack of a simulated environment in which I can practice, and colleagues who are willing to provide feedback; and my inability to couple creative approaches with increased sales.

5. *Develop a timeline that will include periodic meetings with Kate.* Assuming that the initial meeting between us takes place on February 15th, I will meet with Kate on March 12th to report

on what I've learned about different methods for closing deals. On April 30th, I will meet to summarize my first-hand observations of other sales approaches. On May 5th, I will practice various sales approaches in a simulated environment, with colleagues present, to provide feedback. On May 21st, I will meet with Kate to identify those sales approaches that we jointly determine will likely generate increased sales while allowing me to be more creative in my approach.

> **• TIP #42 •**
>
> Successful goal setting hinges on clearly stating the performance objective; breaking the objective down into identifiable and manageable components; isolating resources needed to accomplish each component; identifying possible barriers; and developing a timeline.

Career Development

The third component of the appraisal meeting is, in many respects, the most rewarding. First-time managers quickly learn the importance of keeping employees motivated. Developing a career plan as part of the review process is one important way of doing this.

To maximize results, follow these three steps:

Step One: After discussing future job-related goals, initiate a discussion about the employee's career objectives. Listen, encouraging employees to be as specific as possible. In no way should you try to discourage employees or suggest that their goals are unrealistic or unachievable.

Step Two: Next, ask employees to consider key questions relative to their career goals. These include:

• Is there any formal education or training that may be needed?

- What prior experience is required?
- What prevailing strengths and abilities will help toward the attainment of career goals?
- What developmental opportunities, if any, are available in current positions?
- Is there a correlation between individual career goals and organizational goals?

This last question can be especially meaningful if employees see themselves heading career-wise in a direction that is different from that of their current job. Consider: Could this lack of compatibility impact productivity? Could this adversely affect employer-employee relations? Could this result in frustration on the part of an employee and possibly result in resignation?

Raise these and other related questions before proceeding to the third step. Discussion of these questions can be quite detailed; as such, it might not be completed during the appraisal meeting. For instance, you may want to take some time to explore the plausibility of employees' aspirations. Also, employees may need to research educational requirements. Therefore, follow-up meetings several weeks later are not uncommon.

Step Three: Reconvene with employees and together identify practical steps for implementation in relation to their current jobs and roles within the organization. Together, ensure that the pursuit of career goals does not interfere or conflict with the individual's work performance or goals.

• TIP #43 •

Helping an employee develop a career plan involves three steps: a discussion of the employee's career objectives; consideration of additional education, training, or experience needed; and implementation in relation to the employee's current job.

• 1 1 •

How to Listen Actively

If asked, most of us would probably say that we're good listeners, truly believing that we pay attention when someone speaks. Good listeners would likely answer "No" to the following questions:

- Have you ever been distracted while someone is speaking, to the point of losing track of what she's saying?
- Have you ever tuned out while someone is speaking, because he was just not very interesting?
- Have you ever sworn that someone said something that he maintains never having said?
- Have you ever assumed that you know what a person is going to say before she actually says it?
- Have you ever wished that someone would just stop talking?
- Has anyone every asked you, "Are you listening to me?"?

I don't know of anyone who could honestly say "No" to all of these questions, and it's all right if you didn't—in fact, it makes you pretty much like everyone else. Besides, being a good listener simply means that you are capable of receiving auditory sensations and transmitting them to your brain. That's a capacity we all possess, although some of us exercise that ability more responsibly and thoroughly than others. But being a good listener has no real relation to absorbing the meaning behind words—that is, actively listening—which is what really counts. Tell someone about an incident that happened to you, and he may be able to repeat it word for word. That makes him a good listener. Now, ask him: "Do you see how this incident impacted my career plans? Can you begin to appreciate why I turned down the job offer?" Answering these questions requires the listener to focus on the intent or purpose of the words and makes the speaker feel acknowledged. That's active listening. Being an *active* listener, then, trumps being a *good* listener.

Like any skill, active listening requires practice. You can hone this ability by following some guidelines, balancing the ratio of talking with active listening, and using the power of silence.

• TIP #44 •

Active listening entails absorbing the meaning, intent, and purpose behind a person's words.

Active Listening Guidelines

Active listening is not easy. It requires focus, often when the last thing in the world we feel like doing is putting all of our energy into what a person is saying. Make that a person who speaks in a monotone, is difficult to understand, or is going on at length about a subject that's boring, and the experience can be quite challenging. Even if the person is interesting, active listening requires that we temporarily stop mentally juggling lists of all that needs to be done and concentrate entirely on the speaker.

To maximize your ability to actively listen, follow these guidelines:

• *Concentrate on themes, not words.* Jerry wants his manager, Mackenzie, to understand that the reason his performance is below par is due to "circumstances beyond my control." He explains, "Ever since the new information system was installed, I can't get my work done on time. I'm telling you, that system is out to get me! I can't believe that missing the training sessions on how to work the new program could make that much of a difference. And that wasn't my fault, either. My vacation was planned well in advance, and there was no way I could miss out on going to Italy. That's been my dream for the last five years. Sure, I could have attended the make-up summary class when I got back, but who had the time? You know how much work was waiting for me. I mean, if the system is that hard to learn, you should get a refund from the vendor!"

If Mackenzie listened to every word Jerry said, she might very well buy into his rationale for not meeting deadlines and become derailed by his excess verbiage. But by focusing on the underlying theme of Jerry's words—that is, that the reason why Jerry can't get his work in on time is that he didn't learn the new system—Mackenzie can address the real issue, which is Jerry's ineffective performance.

• *Summarize periodically to ensure a clear picture of what the employee is telling you, and then seek verification.* Not everyone starts at the beginning and provides complete information before moving on to the next thought. You have to concentrate on the pieces of information, pull it all together mentally, and then verbalize what you've heard, both to ensure accuracy and to let the employee know that you're actively listening: "So, Jerry, what you're saying is that the reason you can't get your work in on time is because the new system is too hard to learn; is that correct?"

• *Filter out distractions to avoid missing important information.* While Jerry is making his case for missing deadlines due to the excessive difficulty of the new information system, Mackenzie could easily become distracted by thoughts, including those concerning past discussions with the vendor, how other employees have adjusted to the new program, and Jerry's overall performance. She might also be sidetracked by Jerry's increasingly agitated body language or the noise outside her office. Forcing herself to focus exclusively on Jerry's explanation will enable Mackenzie to listen more actively.

• *Screen out personal biases.* Jerry has made it known of late that he thinks he should be promoted to the recent position created by his manager's promotion. This causes Mackenzie some angst, since she used to work alongsideside Jerry and knows, first hand, some of his shortcomings, including rationalization. She knows that she needs to focus on the issue at hand: that is, Jerry is missing deadlines—and thus determine the cause. She can only do this by actively listening and screening out any personal biases or preconceived notions.

• *Acknowledge any unusual emotional states that could influence your ability to concentrate.* Maybe you had a falling-out with a colleague this morning, found out that the bid on that house you'd hoped to buy fell through, or sat in traffic for two hours en route to work. Incidents such as these can alter your emotional state and can impact your ability to listen actively. If you find that you're stressed or experiencing any other heightened emotion, try to compartmentalize; that is, narrow your field of attention until all that remains are the employee and issues relating to that person. No other person or venue exists. Period. It's hard, but doable.

> **• TIP #45 •**
>
> To maximize your ability to listen actively, concentrate on themes, not words; summarize periodically to ensure a clear picture of what the employee is telling you; filter out distractions; screen out personal biases; and acknowledge any unusual emotional states that could influence your ability to concentrate.

Talking and Active Listening

Many managers need to better balance the amount of talking they do with active listening. This is especially true when it comes to performance-appraisal meetings where many managers talk entirely too much, erroneously believing that they're more in control of the meeting as long as they're doing most of the talking. They become especially chatty when there are performance problems, or they anticipate a negative reaction from an employee concerning her review.

The fact of the matter is, you can't talk and listen actively at the same time. Even if you think you can, the perception on the part of the employee is likely to be that you're not focused on what she's saying.

Try to devote no more than 25 percent of the meeting time to talking, regardless of the content or quality of the review. This percentage of time should be spent highlighting and asking questions about the employee's past performance and success in achieving previously set performance objectives. In addition, you should ask questions and offer guidance with regard to the employee's new performance objectives and career-development plans. The remaining 75 percent of the meeting should be devoted to active listening.

Thought Speed

To better achieve this balance between talking and active listening, practice "thought speed." Researchers have determined that most people think at a rate of approximately 400 words per minute; we speak at a rate of approximately 125 words per minute. Simply translated, we think faster than we speak. That means that while employees are talking, you can use thought speed to:

- Prepare your next question or comment
- Analyze what the employee has said thus far
- Piece together what the employee is saying now in relation to something said at another time
- Glance down at the completed performance-review form and associated documentation to verify information

- Observe the employee's body language (Chapter 12)
- Mentally check your own body language to ensure that you're conveying active listening (Chapter 12)

Thought speed can also work against you. For example, if you anticipate how an employee is likely to respond to a question, jump to conclusions before the employee finishes her statement because your thoughts are racing ahead, or have a mindset about what the employee is going to say, based on previous conversations or past reviews, it's going to be difficult to listen actively to what's really going on.

Coupling thought speed with the guidelines mentioned in Chapter 10 about the approximate amount of time to spend on each of the three main topics in the appraisal meeting (roughly twenty minutes each for past performance, goals, and career development) should better enable managers to adhere to the 75/25 guideline of active listening in relation to talking.

> ### • TIP #46 •
>
> During the performance-appraisal meeting, try to allocate no more than 25 percent of the time to talking, devoting the remainder of time to active listening.

The Power of Silence

Many of us are unnerved by silence. Consider these common scenarios: You're in an elevator, riding from the lobby to the fiftieth floor—no one says a word; you're eating at a restaurant with three of your colleagues—no one speaks; you're driving to work with your carpool buddies—a journey that takes about an hour—in complete silence. In these and other similar circumstances, we typically become agitated, try to think of something witty to say, or come up with a question—anything to generate a human sound and trigger a conversation.

This reaction to silence is eloquently expressed by Estragon, the soulful character in Samuel Beckett's *Waiting for Godot*, as he laments, "In the meantime, let us try and converse calmly, since we are incapable of keeping silent." So powerful is silence.

Instead of viewing silence as a negative, you can use it to bolster your active listening skills. Begin by seeing silence as a means to an end; that is, an opportunity to learn more about an employee's views concerning his past performance, goals, or career-development plans. This will occur because so many people are uncomfortable with silence. In fact, even a few seconds without conversation can make people fidget. If you don't talk, it's likely that the employee will. While technically we no longer have silence, since one person is talking, there is no dialogue in a setting that typically calls for two-way communication. That, alone, can be disarming.

Let's look at how silence can work, by revisiting the appraisal meeting between Jerry and Mackenzie:

As you recall, Jerry wants to convince Mackenzie that the reason why his performance is below par is due to "circumstances beyond his control." That is, he blames his inability to get his work done on time on the company's new information system. Mackenzie knows this isn't the case. Telling him, however, is likely to make Jerry defensive and all the more determined to prove his case. Mackenzie is hoping that, by employing silence, Jerry will ultimately take responsibility for his shortcoming as the first step toward improved performance. Before this is likely to occur, however, Jerry is probably going to need to carry on a bit more, rationalizing as to how the new system is the reason why he can't get his work done on time. As long as he's not behaving in an offensive or inappropriate manner, Mackenzie can allow him some latitude in this regard, remaining completely silent while he rambles. Soon, three things are likely to occur, in this order:

- Jerry is going to become aware of the fact that Mackenzie is not responding.
- He's going to become increasingly cognizant of his own words.

- He's going to hear his words from Mackenzie's perspective.

Mackenzie will know that Jerry has reached the third stage via a combination of factors, including a change in his body language and a faltering conviction in his voice. Now, she can comment with something like "Jerry, I understand that you view the new information system as challenging: Is it possible, however, that you might have done more to learn and adjust to its workings?"

At this point, Jerry and Mackenzie can engage in a dialogue that might not have been as productive, or even possible, prior to Jerry's monologue.

The length of time during which managers remain silent is generally no more than a couple of minutes. With practice, you can become equally comfortable speaking or remaining silent.

• TIP #47 •

Instead of viewing silence as a negative, you can use it to bolster your active listening skills by seeing silence as a means to an end; that is, an opportunity to learn more about an employee's thoughts concerning his past performance, goals, or career-development plans.

• 1 2 •

How to Act: The Importance of Body Language

Managers and employees can learn as much about one another through their body language as from verbal messages. In fact, experts assert that, as much of 55 percent of communication is nonverbal. Verbal messages are considered less persuasive than nonverbal ones; hence, when there is a discrepancy between the verbal and the nonverbal, the nonverbal is often more influential.

Nonverbal communication, or "body language," involves physical movement and gestures, called "kinesics," as well as facial expressions and eye contact. There are a limitless number of possible messages that can be communicated through body language.

Nonverbal messages are easily misinterpreted, generally when translated according to the receiver's own gestures and expressions. For example, you may have a tendency to avoid eye contact when you're hiding something, but that doesn't mean that an employee is avoiding your eyes for the same reason.

Each of us has our own pattern of body language consisting of numerous factors. Together, these factors "speak" to another person from the very first moment of contact.

During performance reviews, you should strive to accomplish three goals: Convey positive body language; accurately assess employees' nonverbal messages; and project consistency between verbal and nonverbal messages.

• TIP #48 •

Verbal messages are considered less persuasive than nonverbal ones; hence, when there is a discrepancy between the verbal and the nonverbal, the nonverbal is often more influential.

Effective Nonverbal Messages

Each of us has our own nonverbal pattern that may be consistently and accurately translated if observed over a period of time. Unfortunately, we tend to react rather than assess; presume to know rather than learn and confirm something to be true. By quickly assigning specific meaning to gestures, movements, and expressions, we often respond to false assumptions. Case in point: the manager who arrives late at work and doesn't have time to prepare for an important presentation to senior management because he has an employee waiting for her annual performance review. She's a good worker, but he's impatient for the meeting to end. As she speaks, he's unaware that he's shaking his head from side to side—a body movement that he exhibits when stressed, as if to jar loose the multiple thoughts in his head. Unknowingly, he's expressing a movement that is typically taken to show disagreement or disbelief. The employee becomes increasingly agitated, not understanding what could cause her manager to disagree so strongly with what she's saying. She begins to stammer and wring her hands, a gesture that the manager finds distracting and annoying. Within minutes, any meaningful dialogue between manager and employee is lost in a sea of misinterpreted body language, resulting in a nonproductive performance-appraisal meeting and harmed employer-employee relations.

You can avoid unfortunate scenarios such as this. Although

we each have unique nonverbal patterns, there are certain gestures and body movements that are almost always interpreted
as having a particular meaning. These are known as "affect displays." They are body movements that are commonly interpreted. You can consciously choose and differentiate between
those that typically reveal positive and negative messages,
striving to convey those that are encouraging, and concealing
any that may be perceived as unconstructive or derogatory.

• TIP #49 •

We often respond to false assumptions by quickly assigning specific
meaning to gestures, movements, and expressions.

Positive Body Language

Cultural influences aside, let's consider some expressions, gestures, and body movements that, in and of themselves, consistently communicate a positive message:

- Direct eye contact
- Erect posture
- Hands held with palms turned upward, resting on the
  desk
- Hands loosely clasped together, resting on the desk
- Head tilted slightly to one side
- Leaning forward in one's seat as the other person speaks
- Nodding the head up and down
- Sitting at an appropriate distance from the other person
  (approximately three feet)
- Sitting at eye level with the other person
- Sitting near the front of the seat
- Smiling
- Keeping one's arms and legs uncrossed

The messages expressed via these examples of positive body
language include: acceptance; approval; attentiveness; encour-

agement; focus; interest; involvement; listening; openness; re-
assurance; responsiveness; sincerity; and understanding. It's
less important that employees be able to distinguish with absolute certainty what message the manager is conveying than it
is for them to know that the expression is a positive one.

Alone, each of these gestures and movements can send a
strong message; combined, the potential impact is even greater.
For instance, imagine sitting across from a manager who is leaning forward, hands clasped together, nodding his head up and
down. Is there any doubt that he is conveying a positive message?
How about the manager who has erect posture, maintains eye
contact, and smiles. Again, this is most certainly going to be interpreted by an employee as expressing a positive response.

The effectiveness of these positive expressions can turn sour,
however, if they are displayed either too intently or for too long.
Direct eye contact, for example, can quickly be perceived as star-
ing or glaring, thereby going from positive body language to
something threatening, hostile, or aggressive. Smiling conveys a
positive message if it is a simple smile; once the smile becomes
a broad smirk, it may be viewed as insincere or mocking, especially if it is out of sync with what the employee is saying.

> **· TIP #50 ·**
>
> Alone, positive gestures and movements can send a strong message;
> combined, the potential impact is even greater.

Negative Body Language

As with positive body language, there are certain gestures,
movements, and expressions that typically convey negative
messages. (The same caveat concerning cultural influences applies.) Here's a list of probable negative body language along
with some characteristic interpretations:

- Ankles crossed: apprehension
- Arms folded across the chest: defensiveness
- Flaring nostrils: anger or frustration

- Head resting in hand: boredom
- Looking down, face turned away: disbelief
- Narrowing of eyes: disagreement, resentment, anger, or disapproval
- Pinching the bridge of one's nose: negative evaluation
- Raising of eyebrows: disbelief or surprise
- Rubbing one's eye: doubt or disbelief
- Scratching one's head: bewilderment
- Shaking one's head from side to side: disagreement or disbelief
- Shifting in one's seat: restlessness or boredom
- Sitting with legs crossed, foot kicking slightly: boredom
- Squinting: disapproval
- Tapping or drumming of fingers: impatience
- Touching, slightly rubbing one's nose: rejection or doubt

You can avoid exhibiting these and other typically negative gestures, movements, and expressions with a little forethought. As with positive body language, the employee might not know exactly what emotion you're displaying, but it is more than likely that he will accurately interpret it as being negative. Therefore, avoiding the nonverbal gestures and movements on this list during performance assessments is advisable.

Mixed Body Language

You are responsible for conveying unambiguous nonverbal communication. Sometimes, though, you may inadvertently convey a conflicting message. For example, body movements such as finger- or foot-tapping can contradict physical movements such as hands held with palms turned upward. Just what is this manager "saying"? Tapping is a gesture that is typically interpreted as impatience; holding one's hands with palms turned upward is a gesture that is commonly taken to mean that the person is responsive or open to what the speaker is expressing. These two movements are out of sync with one another.

When you convey mixed nonverbal messages such as these, the employee on the receiving end typically responds in one of two ways: (1) she will react to one nonverbal message more strongly than the other; or (2) she will be perplexed and focus on the contradicting messages, thereby missing important verbal communication that may also be going on simultaneously. In either case, inaccurate communication is likely to be the end result.

You should, therefore, be aware of how certain gestures, movements, and facial expressions are typically interpreted, striving at all times to exhibit those that are generally considered positive, steering clear of nonverbal communication that will probably be viewed as negative, and avoiding conflicting messages. One way to avoid the latter is to try to understand how employees are responding; that is, to interpret their body language accurately.

• TIP #51 •

You are responsible for conveying unambiguous nonverbal communication.

Accurately Interpreting Body Language

We all habitually exhibit certain nonverbal behaviors without realizing it: jiggling coins in our pocket, nibbling at our nails, or twirling our hair when tense or anxious, for example, are movements that some of us may unconsciously display. These nonverbal expressions are called *adaptors*, and can speak volumes about how we're feeling or what we're thinking.

An individual's adaptors are revealing. Attentive managers can use these unique, nonverbal behaviors of each employee to identify specific patterns. For example, the employee who rubs his eyes every time you broach the subject of how he's doing with a current long-term project is conveying a pattern that suggests that something is amiss. It's likely that this individual rubs his eyes whenever he's uncomfortable or feels he's being pressed to discuss something he'd prefer to avoid. This pattern alerts you to the fact that you need to probe deeper and persist until you determine what's really going on.

It is significant to note that the same body movement may mean something entirely different when executed by another person. In the example given, it is not so much the actual act of rubbing one's eyes that is significant as much as the pattern of when the employee rubs her eyes and what else is going on each time the gesture occurs.

Sometimes, gestures and expressions that are commonly interpreted to mean something positive can mean just the opposite. It would be great if body language accurately alerted us to levels of, say, preparedness or honesty, but a hasty misinterpretation of gestures, body movements, or facial expressions can spell disaster.

Here's how: Let's say an employee enters your office for her annual performance-appraisal meeting. The review you've prepared is mixed, in that she has a spotty attendance record and her attention to detail is barely acceptable. When it comes time to recap the first of these two areas, you remind her of how important it is that she meet her obligation to arrive on time and not leave before she's supposed to. As you speak, she leans forward, tilts her head slightly to one side, and nods up and down. These are all positive nonverbal movements that you take to mean understanding, agreement, and future compliance. Now, you reference her lack of attention to detail. The employee repeats the same set of nonverbal movements. Good: You've reiterated your concern, and she has indicated, via a pattern of positive body language, that her performance will improve. Unfortunately, you've forgotten that during past coaching and counseling sessions the employee has consistently demonstrated this same pattern of nonverbal behavior; that is, leaning in, tilting, and nodding. Yet, nothing has changed in terms of her performance.

Whether deliberate or unconscious, this employee demonstrates what is typically considered positive body language to convey something quite different: Nonverbally, she appears to commit to changing her behavior, but in actuality she has not.

When assessing an individual's adaptors, explore the circumstances under which they are exhibited. In addition to looking for common denominators, consider cause and effect; that is, as a result of this nonverbal display, here's what has and has not happened. If there's a pattern over time, then you can feel reasonably safe in assuming that you can accurately interpret that person's body language.

> **• TIP #52 •**
>
> Accurately assess nonverbal messages conveyed by an employee by identifying individual patterns over time.

Consistency Between Nonverbal and Verbal Messages

In addition to body language that is typically interpreted and individual patterns of behavior, many people respond to *illustrators*: movements and gestures that add meaning to a verbal message. For example, when delivering a seminar, a speaker might jab at the air as a matter of emphasis. If she made this same gesture without speaking, no one would have a clue as to what she was doing.

Illustrators, then, do not have a specific meaning that can be pinpointed; rather, they serve to support a person's words, providing consistency between nonverbal and verbal messages.

Project Consistency

Strive to use illustrators to support what you are saying, being careful not to use gestures, movements, or expressions that will conflict. Such a conflict between verbal and nonverbal messages can be confusing, leaving the receiver to wonder which message is more accurate.

To project consistency between nonverbal and verbal messages, concentrate on using clear language supported by typically interpreted gestures. For example, if you want to express encouragement, you could say, "I think your goal of becoming a supervisor is achievable; let's talk about what you need to do to get there." At the same time, maintain direct eye contact, smile, and sit up straight in your chair, conveying a readiness to discuss the employee's interest in upward mobility.

Seek Consistency

You should also look for consistency between the nonverbal and verbal information you are receiving from employees. Here's a scenario that illustrates how this might work: Chloe is meeting with her manager, Helene, to discuss her annual performance appraisal. A preliminary examination of her review reveals what she expected: consistently high ratings in every category. As Helene delves into the details of each area, her body language is supportive and encouraging, including direct eye contact and leaning forward. When Chloe speaks, Helene nods, indicating understanding. When it comes time to discuss Chloe's future aspirations, Helene listens carefully and then says, "I hear what you're saying, Chloe, about wanting to continue growing in your current position, but I can't help but wonder if there isn't something more you'd like to accomplish."

Helene is responding to the inconsistency between Chloe's body language and her words. Specifically, the fact that she shifted in her seat and hunched over when the subject turned to her career objectives. Helene doesn't assign a specific meaning to either movement; however, the sudden change in Chloe's body language sends a message to Helene that something is amiss. Sure enough, Chloe straightens up in her seat and cautiously begins to describe her ultimate career goal. Helene is careful to convey positive body language coupled with encouraging verbal language as Chloe gains greater confidence and reveals more details about her dream job.

• TIP #53 •

Illustrators do not have a specific meaning that can be pinpointed; rather, they serve to support a person's words, providing consistency between nonverbal and verbal messages.

How to Handle Challenging Performance-Appraisal Situations

"The best-laid plans of mice and men often go awry" is a famous line adapted from "To a Mouse," by Robert Burns. (The actual line reads, "The best-laid schemes o' mice an' men gang aft agley," but that doesn't have quite the same ring.) It is commonly interpreted to mean that no matter how carefully we plan, something may still go wrong. At the risk of being accused of inappropriately waxing poetic, I suggest that this line applies to those who have diligently prepared for the performance review, only to find that the meeting does not proceed as anticipated, due to unexpected employee behavior.

Coaching and counseling throughout the evaluation period should enable you to develop a fairly solid sense of how employees are likely to respond to an appraisal. Still, unexpected responses can occur. If the responses are unexpected, how can managers prepare for them? In a word: anticipation. That is, expect and prepare for the unexpected. No matter how well you believe you know an employee, you never know, with absolute certainty, what may trigger an unexpected reaction.

In Chapter 9, we observed Russell reviewing questions to ask himself in order to maximally provide his employee, Jill, with a fair and objective evaluation. Russell's self-examination soliloquy includes: "Am I prepared for the possible reactions of the employee?" Russell understands that while he can anticipate how Jill is likely to respond, it's helpful to know that there are six frequently displayed employee behavior patterns exhibited during performance-appraisal meetings. Familiarization with these behaviors, recommended approaches for dealing with them, and potential outcomes will enable him to be better prepared for any response.

> ### • TIP #54 •
>
> Coaching and counseling throughout the evaluation period should enable you to develop a fairly solid sense of how employees are likely to respond to an appraisal. Still, unexpected responses can occur.

Possible Employee Reactions to Performance Reviews

We'll reference Russell and Jill as we illustrate six typically displayed employee-behavior patterns exhibited during performance-appraisal meetings. Recommended approaches and potential outcomes will follow later in the chapter.

Agreement

Initially, it may seem that having an employee who agrees with your evaluation, whether positive or negative, is the perfect scenario. But a closer look will reveal that having an agreeable employee is not as ideal as one might think.

We observe that Russell has rated Jill's ability to meet deadlines as "exceeds expectations." That's the highest rating possible. The rest of Jill's appraisal is equally outstanding, and Jill's reply to all of this is "Sounds good to me!" That's an understandable response to a glowing evaluation. Consider, though, what would happen if Russell were to rate Jill as "requiring improvement" when it comes to generating new business. As

an agreeable employee, she might reply, "Yes. You're absolutely right." Their exchange might then go something like this:

Russell: You agree that you require improvement when it
comes to generating new business?

Jill: If you say I do, then I do.

Russell: What do you see yourself doing to generate new
business?

Jill: Whatever you want me to do.

Russell: Jill, it's not for me to tell you what to do—I'm asking what you think about what you can do to generate new
business.

Jill: You're the boss—I'll do whatever you think it will take
to improve.

You get the idea.

Argument

Argumentative employees are likely to disagree with individual competency ratings and, if less than perfect, their overall
evaluations as well. Simply stated, they refuse to accept your
evaluation of their work. Despite supporting information, they
may fabricate evidence to show that any hint of a negative review is inaccurate. Dialogue between an argumentative employee and her manager might go something like this:

Russell: I'm sure this comes as no surprise to you, Jill; we've
talked about your inability to meet deadlines before, and
you've acknowledged that you need to work harder to get your
work in on time.

Jill: Sure, I said that; what was I supposed to say? I wasn't
about to shoot myself in the foot by disagreeing with you.

Russell: But you're disagreeing now?

Jill: I disagree that I have to work harder; actually, I have to
work less hard. I've been covering for Elaine. Personal problems made her fall behind, and I've been doing her work so she
wouldn't get into trouble.

Russell: This is the first I'm hearing about this. Are you saying you did her work in addition to your own?

Jill: I thought I could manage both jobs, but even if I missed a few of my own deadlines, I knew I could handle things better than she could; she's just not as strong-willed as I am.

Defensiveness

Defensive employees are overly concerned with self-protection and are quick to transfer blame to others. In addition, they tend to react emotionally to statements regarding areas requiring improvement, despite specific examples. This emotional reaction can include breaking down in tears, becoming verbally abusive, and storming out of the appraisal meeting. Here are Russell and Jill, illustrating varied defensive responses:

Russell: Jill, let's talk about one of your goals from last year; that is, to make fewer mistakes.

Jill: I know what you're going to say!

Russell: Do you? What?

Jill: I didn't meet my goal. You're right; I didn't. But it wasn't my fault! If you were doing your job as manager, you'd know that! [verbal abuse]

Russell: We set that goal together during your last review; it's a goal that you said was achievable.

Jill: I thought it was at the time; but then I got sick, and when I came back to work I was really tired all the time, and each time I went to check my work, my computer crashed, because it's so old and slow, and maybe if I had a better system I could get more work done, and . . . [tears]

Russell: Jill, where do you suggest we go from here?

Jill: We? I don't know about *you*, but *I* don't need this; I'm *out of here!* [Jill abruptly ends the meeting and leaves]

Nervousness

Some employees are highly anxious about expressing themselves. They hem and haw, worried about their manager's reaction to different ideas or opinions. Some may second-guess themselves to the extent that they experience panic attacks. For them, performance-appraisal meetings can be upsetting, even when they're being praised.

Russell: Let's talk about your problem-solving ability. How would you rate yourself?

Jill: Um, good, I guess.

Russell: Tell me more.

Jill: Um, well, it's good . . . I guess; that is, do you think it's good?

Russell: I think you're doing a fine job, but I'd like to hear more from you.

Jill: Thank you! Well, it just comes naturally for me.

Russell: Why do you think that's so?

Jill: Uh, because . . . it's just easy for me; I'm glad you agree.

Overconfidence

Overconfident employees never seem to tire of telling everyone that they're assets to the organization. They seem unaware of, or unconcerned about, any deficiencies, and as such, they have difficulty acknowledging ways in which they might improve their performance. Instead, they insist on receiving a promotion or raise. In addition, they tend to be highly critical of feedback from others.

Russell: I'd like to review some of the feedback I received from our client, H. H. Hunter, as part of our 360-degree evaluation program.

Jill: Shoot!

Russell: Overall, they were pleased with the service you provided.

Jill: I'm not surprised to hear that.

Russell: They also indicated that, at times, you seemed preoccupied and unresponsive to their needs.

Jill: Impossible.

Russell: Impossible?

Jill: Absolutely. I was completely at their disposal. If anyone was unresponsive, it was the lead technician on the job. Look, the fact of the matter is that I did that job better than anyone could have expected. I should get a hefty raise as well as a promotion for putting up with that incompetent technician.

Silence

Regardless of what you say or ask, silent employees typically respond with nods, shrugs, or monosyllabic statements. They fail to actively participate in their own evaluation process. This can be both frustrating and counterproductive.

Russell: Now that I've gone through each category on the appraisal form and offered my assessment of your work, I'd like to hear what you have to say.

Jill: It's fine.

Russell: Fine? What about the areas in which I indicated you need improvement?

Jill: They're fine.

Russell: What, specifically, can you do to increase your speed?

Jill: I dunno.

Russell: What resources could you tap into?

Jill: [shrug . . . sigh . . .]

• TIP #55 •

There are six employee behavior patterns that employees typically exhibit during performance-appraisal meetings: agreement; argument; defensiveness; nervousness; overconfidence; and silence.

Recommended Approaches

These six illustrated employee-behavior patterns can present quite a challenge for the unsuspecting first-time manager. With a little bit of advance thought and preparation, however, performance-appraisal meetings with employees exhibiting these behaviors can become not only manageable, but productive encounters.

We'll revisit Russell as he meets with Jill, exhibiting these six employee reactions, to see how he might alter his approach with each scenario:

Agreement

Encourage overly agreeable employees to discuss their self-evaluations, point by point, before you share your assessment. Then, ask them to discuss their views concerning future goals and career development before offering your thoughts.

Russell might say, "Before I go over how I rated your performance, I'd like to hear how you rated yourself. As we go through each category, tell me not only how you evaluated yourself, but also your rationale for each rating. Let's begin with how you view your ability to meet deadlines."

Russell might then continue, "Jill, we've explored your past performance; now, let's look ahead. Why don't you begin by describing your future goals; then, we'll talk about your interests with regard to career development."

Argument

You can afford to allow for a certain amount of disagreement as long as the dialogue remains constructive. Actively listen for the essence of what the employee is saying, and seek clarification to help determine any hidden, underlying causes for the argumentative behavior. Begin by summarizing what the employee has said thus far. This will let the employee know that you've been listening, ensure understanding, and allow her to hear how her words sound coming from you.

Russell might say, Jill, I want to make certain I understand you correctly: You agreed that you needed to work on meeting deadlines, but you only said that because you did not want me to know you were covering for Elaine's inability to complete her assignments. Furthermore, you felt you could do both your job and hers successfully, but that if you missed a few deadlines it was no big deal. Is that correct?"

Defensiveness

As with argumentative employees, you can allow a certain display of defensiveness as you actively listen to determine the real issue at hand. Address the person's performance, and not her personality; and whatever you do, avoid taking anything personally. This will allow you to remain objective and stay focused.

After Jill rambled on about why she failed to make fewer mistakes, Russell could interject, "Jill, I need to ask you to slow down and back up somewhat. I'm hearing you say a great deal about factors that interfered with your ability to improve on your error factor, but I'm still not clear as to just what's going on. Let's try this: I'm going to ask a specific question; you provide a succinct answer. Here's the question: *What is the main reason you continue to make an excessive number of mistakes?"*

Nervousness

If you sense that an employee is nervous, begin by briefly explaining the purpose of the meeting and how it will benefit her. Initially discuss areas that she knows best and is most comfortable talking about. Ask for her opinion regarding specific issues, and inquire about her areas of interest. Sometimes it's best to begin with a discussion of career objectives.

Here's how Russell might begin: "Jill, the purpose of a performance appraisal is to help employees fully utilize their skills, knowledge, and interests. We'll talk a bit about your past performance and how successful you've been in achieving past goals. We'll also look ahead and discuss future goals and your career objectives. In fact, why don't we start with the end: I'm interested in learning more about your career objectives. As I recall, you've expressed an interest in becoming more actively involved with our human resources information system; tell me about that."

Overconfidence

All employees have areas in which they can improve; overconfident employees sometimes need to be reminded of this simple fact. They also need to understand that feedback of a corrective nature is not necessarily criticism. Present a balanced picture of strengths and areas requiring improvement accompanied by specific, documented, supporting examples.

Russell could say, "The feedback I received from H. H. Hunter contained some high praise for your creative marketing ability. They also indicated that, at times, you seemed preoccupied and unresponsive to their needs. Here are some of the specifics they provided."

Silence

Encourage these individuals to talk about areas with which they are familiar and comfortable. Consider, too, talking about general topics, such as ideal work environments. Then, relate their reactions to their current jobs, and ask them to identify common denominators.

Russell could approach Jill by saying, "Jill, before we get into the particulars of your review, I was wondering how, after being here for a year now, the job measures up to your expectations. During our interview I recall asking you to describe your ideal job. What is there in your work that fits in with that idyllic description?"

> **• TIP #56 •**
>
> Performance-appraisal meetings with employees who exhibit unexpected traits can become productive encounters.

Potential Outcomes

What's likely to happen if you anticipate possible employee reactions and alter your approach to the performance-appraisal meeting by allowing for differing responses? Potentially, a great deal:

• *Agreeable Employees.* Agreeable employees will have the opportunity to express previously unvoiced feeling and opinions, thereby allowing managers to understand their interests better. It could also ensure a greater commitment to defining and meeting specific career goals.

• *Argumentative Employees.* While it's easy to become annoyed with an argumentative employee, try viewing this as an opportunity to clear the air. It may be that these individuals are frustrated in their current positions but haven't identified what it is they'd prefer doing. If you remain calm and reasonable, expressing interest in what the employee has to say, there's greater opportunity for a healthy dialogue.

• *Defensive Employees.* Addressing a person's performance, rather than her personality, will allow you to help reduce the employee's level of defensiveness and achieve greater objectivity.

• *Nervous Employees:* Focusing on areas that the nervous employee knows best and feels most comfortable talking about is likely to have a calming effect on the individual, thereby opening lines of communication.

• *Overconfident Employees:* Presenting a balanced picture of strengths and areas requiring improvement accompanied by specific, documented, supporting examples may enable overconfident employees to assess their own performance more realistically.

• *Silent Employees:* Encouraging shy employees to talk about areas with which they are familiar and comfortable should encourage a dialogue and allow you to focus on their performance.

• TIP #57 •

Developing a keener understanding of employee goals is one possible outcome of accommodating differing responses to a performance appraisal.

Disciplinary Action

Performance appraisals may lay the foundation for, and thus lead to, disciplinary action, including termination, despite your best efforts to help an employee improve performance or behavior.

The following steps are intended as a guide for most kinds of infractions, such as excessive tardiness or absenteeism. Certain serious occurrences, such as acts of physical violence, may warrant suspension without pay, pending an investigation, or immediate dismissal.

Verbal Warning

Verbal warnings should always be conducted in private and should serve as opportunities to clarify misunderstood directions and eliminate incorrect assumptions.

First Written Warning

If the same problem recurs after a verbal warning, issue a written warning. This is a statement of what has occurred, who was involved, when and where the unacceptable behavior took place, why it warrants disciplinary action, and what improvement is expected in the future. Both verbally and in writing, give the employee an opportunity to read the written warning and make comments. Then, ask the employee to sign the written warning, indicating that he understands its contents.

Second Written Warning

If the problem is repeated or continues, it may result in a second written warning. If this occurs, the guidelines described under "First Written Warning" should be reapplied.

Suspension

If the problem continues, suspension may be warranted. A suspension is usually for a period of one to three working days and without pay. Explain the reasons for the suspension, and warn the employee that failure to improve in work or conduct could result in termination.

Termination

After a verbal warning, two written warnings, and a suspension, termination for repeated or continued infractions may be warranted. A written statement summarizing the reasons for termination should be placed in the employee's HR file.

• TIP #58 •

Performance appraisals may lay the foundation for, and thus lead to, disciplinary action, including termination, despite your best efforts to help an employee improve performance or behavior.

•14•

How to Avoid Typical Performance-Appraisal Pitfalls

By periodically reviewing typical performance appraisal pitfalls you're likely to conduct more successful reviews and enjoy maximally productive working relationships with your employees.

Legal Pitfalls

No one expects you to be a legal expert; however, the Equal Employment Opportunity Commission (EEOC) and other legislative bodies expect you to be familiar with, and able to implement, relevant legislation as it pertains to all aspects of employment, including performance appraisals. Appendix B identifies relevant federal legislation. State and local laws may differ and should also be considered.

Discriminatory Language

The law is clear when it comes to using discriminatory language in the performance-appraisal process: Simply stated, don't do it. This caveat pertains to overt racial epithets and denigrating sexual language, as well as any direct or indirect reference to age, gender, race, national origin, disability, or sexual orientation. Beyond these obvious references are those that are subtler, but just as hazardous, when it comes to being considered discriminatory. Indeed, language that initially appears innocuous may still be considered biased and therefore actionable. Here are some examples from written reviews:

- Ella's coworkers have described her as pushy when it comes to working on projects, but I think that's just a reflection of her ethnicity.
- If Rose wants to get ahead, she's going to have to learn to play ball with the guys.
- Sam does his job well; however, he needs to keep up with the younger workers when it comes to his technical skills.
- J. J. shows great promise; unfortunately, because of his religious beliefs, he's unable to join the others when they celebrate a successful project with an after-work social drink. That could hurt his chances for advancement.
- Barb has great people skills, but needs to pay more attention to her appearance and lose some weight. Customers are hesitant to buy from someone who doesn't look good in the clothes she's trying to sell.

You can avoid being accused of using discriminatory language by focusing on job-related facts, rather than personal characteristics. Here are some examples of performance-related statements that would not be considered discriminatory:

- This job calls for the ability to communicate effectively with members of senior management. On three separate occasions, vice presidents have commented on Jonathan's poor communication skills when making presentations.
- Customer service representatives need to be able to diffuse potentially volatile situations. Richard has consistently demonstrated the ability to calm down irate customers and achieve resolutions that are satisfactory to all concerned.

- Ashley has failed to demonstrate some critical skills that are needed in order to be an effective supervisor: Specifically, she doesn't delegate tasks and exhibits ineffective time-management skills.
- This job requires the ability to multi-task. George regularly balances several tasks and successfully meets all of his deadlines.
- One of Jeremy's responsibilities is to participate in projects as a member of a team. So far, he has demonstrated an unwillingness to support team decisions that are contrary to his own.

Each of these job-related statements should then be supported with specific examples.

> **• TIP #59 •**
>
> The law is clear when it comes to using discriminatory language in the performance-appraisal process: Don't do it. You can avoid being accused of using discriminatory language by focusing on job-related facts, rather than personal characteristics.

Implied Contracts

Be careful not to commit to something that might happen in the future. This is called an "implied contract" and could result in charges of discrimination if what you promised doesn't materialize. For example, suppose you were to say, "Your work is outstanding. I expect to see you taking over my job when I transfer overseas next year." If, when you transfer, that employee is not promoted, the information could be used as the basis of a lawsuit alleging discrimination.

Here are some additional examples of language that could be taken as an implied contract and their legal, amended versions:

- "Who knew, when I hired you a year ago, that you'd turn out to be such a superstar?! *Here's hoping you don't get tired of us and take your talents elsewhere!"* (The language of this statement could be amended as follows: "Who knew, when I hired you a year ago, that you'd turn out to be such a superstar?! *Your performance thus far has been outstanding."*)

- "Chris, I know you've heard some talk about reductions in staff. *I just want to assure you that as long as I have anything to say about it, your job is secure."* (The language of this statement could be amended as follows: "Chris, I know you've heard some talk about reductions in staff. *I'll be sure to let you know as soon as I learn anything concrete."*)

- "I want you to know that I plan on recommending you for a promotion to senior analyst; that is, of course, assuming your work continues to be as excellent as it has been to date." (The language of this statement could be amended as follows: *"Your work as an analyst has been excellent to date. I'd like to hear about your future aspirations and career goals."*)

• TIP #60 •

Avoid committing to something that might happen in the future. This is called an "implied contract" and could result in charges of discrimination if what you promised doesn't materialize.

The Top-Ten Performance-Appraisal Pitfalls

First-time managers typically fall into ten performance-appraisal pitfalls:

1. Becoming defensive or argumentative.
2. Discussing personality traits and attitudes.
3. Interrupting the employee as long as he or she is saying something relevant.
4. Asking leading questions such as "Don't you think. . . . ?"

and offering advice via statements such as "If I were you. . . ."

5. Making condemning statements such as "I never did that when I had your job."
6. Expressing opinions, impressions, and feelings rather than sticking with the facts.
7. Solving the employee's problems for him or her.
8. Engaging in superficial or irrelevant discussions.
9. Talking about oneself.
10. Talking down to the employee.

If you find yourself falling prey to any these pitfalls, consider taking some preventative steps. For instance, review the job description prior to meeting with an employee as a reminder of the actual standards of performance; view disagreement as part of a healthy exchange; understand that differences in personality and work style can positively contribute to a diverse work environment; and accept the fact that change can be beneficial.

Performance-Appraisal Syndromes

Despite all your efforts and best intentions, it's still possible to be influenced by factors to the extent that they become counterproductive patterns of behavior. When applied to conducting performance appraisals, these patterns may be categorized as specific types of syndromes.

The Good/Bad Past-Performance Syndrome

Perhaps the most influential factor of all is past performance. It's easy to be influenced by good past performance to the extent that you assume that it will always continue. Hence, performance "glitches" tend to be rationalized and overlooked. On the other hand, poor past performance can detract from improved performance, causing you to discount steps toward betterment.

The Recency Syndrome

An extension of the good/bad past-performance issue is the *recency syndrome*. That's where a significant, positive, recent accomplishment stands out, overshadowing an otherwise extensive pattern of poor performance. Likewise, a recent error may stand out in your mind, overriding a year's worth of steady performance.

The "You're the Best" Syndrome

It's all too easy to fall into the trap of comparing employees with one another, thereby granting the "best" of the group the highest possible rating. In reality, that person's performance might warrant no more than an above-average rating, and the others somewhat less. In addition to falling into the comparability trap, this manager has department-wide performance issues to deal with.

The Blind-Spot Syndrome

The *blind-spot syndrome* can also be problematic when it comes time to conduct an appraisal meeting. Here, you may excuse those shortcomings that you exhibit yourself. Honestly evaluating the employee would mean confronting one's own deficiencies—something that many of us have difficulty doing.

The Assumption Syndrome

Then there's the *assumption syndrome,* whereby you may presume to know why there's a change in an employee's level of performance. For example, you could conclude, without any facts to support your contention, that the reason why an excellent worker's performance is starting to slide is attributable to a sick family member; or you might believe that the reason why an average performer is showing signs of improvement is because of your decision to partner him up with a mentor.

The "I Don't Like" Syndrome

You probably have your own personal "I don't like" list that you subconsciously refer to when conducting appraisal meetings. Can you admit to any of the statements on this list?

I don't like employees . . .

- . . . who fail to meet my own personal standards, despite the fact that they meet those identified in the job description.
- . . . who challenge, disagree, or argue with me.
- . . . who are either too independent or dependent, whichever the perceived case may be.
- . . . with personality traits decidedly different from my own or that of the department's top performer.
- . . . whose work style differs from my own when I performed that job.
- . . . who try to change the ways in which tasks traditionally have been performed.
- . . . who work too hard to please me.

• TIP #61 •

Despite all your efforts and best intentions, it's still possible to fall into typical performance-appraisal pitfalls and to be influenced by factors to the extent that they become counterproductive patterns of behavior. When applied to conducting performance appraisals, these patterns may be categorized as specific types of syndromes.

Trying to Remember What to Cover

Avoid trying to commit to memory all that should be covered during a performance-appraisal session. Instead, keep a checklist nearby that identifies key areas. This will ensure full treatment of key areas and allow for a comprehensive exchange between yourself and the employee. Here's what your checklist should consist of:

Summary of Past Performance

While the appraisal form probably has an overall rating that summarizes your assessment of the employee's past performance, it's still advisable to verbalize your overall evaluation. Here are two sample summarizing statements:

- "In summary, I'd like to reiterate how pleased I am with your overall work performance. You exhibit a fine work ethic and are especially impressive when motivating your team to meet deadlines. You should feel proud of all that you've accomplished thus far."
- "We've spent some time talking about your need to improve with regard to accuracy in your work. You've identified some specific steps that you're agreed to implement, and we have a schedule of meetings to discuss your progress. I hope you're as confident as I am that you'll succeed."

Review of Previously Set Performance Objectives

Determining whether the employee has succeeded in meeting previously set performance objectives will enable you both to move forward in setting new objectives. Here are some examples of what you can start with:

- "The manner in which you tackled last year's goals is truly impressive. I'm also pleased to learn that you found the process to be personally gratifying."
- "As far as your success in meeting previously set performance objectives is concerned, I would like to begin by saying that, despite the fact that you fell somewhat short of your overall goal, you exhibited tremendous effort. I want you to know that it did not go unnoticed."

Working Together to Set New Performance Objectives

How well the employee managed to meet past performance objectives sets the stage for setting future goals. This is a joint effort, and you should be able to make a statement similar to the following before concluding the meeting: "I'm pleased with our discussion about your goals for the upcoming year. We have a timeline of interim steps, and we'll meet to discuss your progress as indicated on that timeline. If you have any questions or concerns in between scheduled meetings, please don't hesitate to come see me."

Working with the Employee on a Career-Development Plan

Even the most efficient and dedicated employees are going to feel discouraged if the work they perform does not correlate with their personal career development. Conversely, you need to know that individuals' career plans are connected with the jobs they're performing. Consider this statement before concluding the appraisal meeting: "We've agreed to meet in a week to discuss further your career goal of becoming a key figure in the marketing department. I've given you a career-development form to complete, and I'll do the same. I'm looking forward to being instrumental in helping you achieve your personal objectives while continuing to making contributions to this organization."

Reinforcing Praise and Ending on a Positive Note

Obviously this is easiest to do with outstanding employees. Say, "I'd like to conclude by reiterating what I've said throughout this meeting: You are an asset to this organization in so many ways, especially your ability to work under pressure, your willingness to take on additional tasks to help others meet their deadlines, and the accuracy of your work."

Everyone deserves recognition for whatever it is he or she does well. If there is absolutely nothing you can find to praise, then, as stated earlier, one must wonder why that person is still on the payroll. Here's something you can say to an employee who has numerous performance issues but still performs some tasks well: "Despite the areas in which you need to improve, you continue to demonstrate an in-depth knowledge of the technical aspect of your job; that's impressive."

Delivering Criticism Constructively

Talking about areas in which an employee needs to improve can be less stressful if you strive to be straightforward and specific, provide a balanced picture, and are encouraging.

Here's an example of criticism that is *not* constructive: "We've talked a dozen times about your failure to focus on details. You're just not getting it. I'm worried that the only way I'm going to get through to you is to write you up as part of our formal disciplinary process. Then, maybe you'll understand how serious this is!"

Here's a more productive approach to constructive criticism:"We've talked about your need to be better focused on details. You've identified some steps that you feel will help you achieve this goal, and I support them. Your work in many other areas is commendable; I'm confident that you'll succeed in elevating the level of your attention to detail if you adhere to the plan you've mapped out."

Encouraging Employees to Make Comments and Ask Questions

Performance-evaluation meetings consist of two-way communication. In Chapter 11, we discussed the approximate ratio of talking and listening, determining that you should talk about 25 percent of the time. Remind yourself of this figure throughout the meeting, and at the end ask yourself how successful you were in affording the employee the bulk of the time for commenting or asking questions. Just before ending, try making one of these statements: "Before concluding our meeting, do you have any additional comments or questions?" Or "Are there any questions I didn't ask, or is there anything I didn't cover that you wanted to discuss?

Reiterating Your Availability for Help and Support

Remember that one of your primary responsibilities as a manager is that of a coach, whereby you are available to regularly offer assistance, support, praise, and constructive criticism (Chapter 2). Reiterating this availability to an employee before ending the appraisal meeting can help to enhance employer-employee relations: "This has been a very productive meeting. Please know that my door is open if, at any time, you want to ask a question, share an observation, or talk about any issues you may be having with your work. I'm here to help and support you in any way needed."

• TIP #62 •

Avoid trying to commit to memory all that should be covered during a performance-appraisal session. Instead, keep a checklist nearby, identifying key areas.

How to Conduct Appraisals on Different-Performance-Level Employees

Everyone needs feedback: Average performers need to hear about what they're doing well and how they can continue to develop; top performers need to have their work acknowledged and learn about additional challenges; and marginal performers need guidelines for improvement. In addition, every employee deserves the opportunity to discuss interests and aspirations so managers can consider how individual and organizational goals may coincide.

> **• TIP #63 •**
>
> All employees, regardless of their level of performance, need feedback.

Average Performers

Evaluating average performers can be challenging. They tend to inspire summarizing comments such as "Meets the requirements of the job"; "Acceptable performance"; "Good ability to meet job expectations"; "Regularly performs in a competent manner"; and "Acceptable work," with little verbiage to lend support.

Average performers are not unlike students with a "C" average. And like these C students, average performers sometimes go unnoticed. Think about it: Top performers draw attention to themselves by consistently demonstrating an in-depth understanding of their work and exceeding that which is required; and marginal employees perform work requiring close monitoring and supervision. Average performers, on the other hand, just plod along, generating neither excessive praise nor criticism. They are just there, not bothering anyone, doing their work, day after day, after day, after day.

So, you may wonder, *What's the problem?* Well, it's not so much that there's a problem; rather, it's a matter of ensuring that this large percentage of the employee population isn't overlooked or underutilized.

Average performers are the largest population of most organizations. As such, by virtue of sheer numbers, they form the foundation of any business. Consider: If you had an excessive number of marginal employees, you'd be focusing too intently on correcting behavior; too many top performers, and you'd have a big group requiring continuous challenges and stimuli, lest they leave to work elsewhere.

This is not to say that average employees do not require, or deserve, challenges; nor does it mean that they do not have performance issues that require attention. It's a matter of degree. Average employees are, well, just that: middle-of-the-road when it comes to behavior; and not too demanding with regard to having their needs met.

Words to Describe Average Performers

Since average employees do not cry out for attention, it's no wonder that managers have difficulty evaluating their performance. After all, how many ways can you say, "average"? Well, here's a list of terms that can be used when appraising the work of average employees, each of which requires amplification by way of example:

- Accepts full responsibility for results
- Avoids mistakes and errors
- Can be trusted to complete assignments on time
- Is consistently punctual
- Exercises appropriate cost control
- Gets along well with coworkers
- Gives clear directions
- Is a solid achiever
- Is consistently prepared
- Is cooperative when working with others
- Keeps accurate records
- Lends support as needed
- Manages paperwork effectively
- Regular in attendance
- Reliable
- Supplies necessary support services
- Understands departmental policies
- Uses proven methods and techniques to achieve results
- Works effectively with others
- Works steadily

These statements all reflect performance that is steady and on-going: qualities that managers should harvest and further develop.

Developing Goals

Too often, at the conclusion of a performance-appraisal meeting with an average employee, you might be tempted to state simply, "Keep up the good work." The phrase is meant to be complimentary, but it lacks substance. In essence, what you're saying is "Just keep doing what you've been doing, and next year at this time I'll say the exact same thing."

The emphasis of an appraisal meeting with average em-

ployees should be on the future; that is, on upcoming performance goals. When developing future performance goals,
encourage average employees to stretch beyond what they believe they can achieve. Offer examples of work they've previously performed, to illustrate accomplishments and abilities.
More importantly, ask them to identify at least three personal
attributes with supporting examples.

Consider Billy, an "average" regional sales representative,
and Miranda, his manager, who would like to see him broaden
his scope and accomplish more on the job:

Miranda: Billy, what kind of numbers are you thinking of
setting for next year's sales goals?

Billy: I'm thinking the same as this past year, plus maybe
an additional five percent.

Miranda: That's a good place to begin, Billy, but I'm wondering if you're not selling yourself short with that goal. Tell
me, can you name three attributes of a good sales representative?

Billy: Well, I'd say a sales representative should be persis-
tent, patient, and also a good listener.

Miranda: Agreed. I think you exhibit all of those traits. For
example, when you went after the Monroe account, you were
determined to hang in there till you closed the deal. You listened closely to Monroe's initial objections and countered each
one with a solid argument. Before long, Monroe was signing
papers, and you were closing the deal. Now, can you give me
another example of when you exhibited persistence, patience,
and good listening?

Miranda's goal is to get Billy to acknowledge his own skills
and strengths so that he'll be motivated to achieve a higher
level of performance. It's not so much that her objective is to
make him a top performer; rather, it is to ensure that he's performing to the best of his ability.

> **• TIP #64 •**
>
> Average performers are the largest population of most organizations. As such, by virtue of sheer numbers, they form the foundation of any business and should not be ignored when it comes to performance appraisals.

Top Performers

Top performers typically constitute somewhere around one-fifth of an organization's population. From a productivity, growth, and brainpower perspective, the top 20 percent of any group is critical. In addition, these are the employees who are very difficult to replace. Hence, it's important to ensure that they don't get bored, burn out, or quickly plateau.

When it comes to evaluating top performers, your primary objective is to keep them challenged. Many top performers thrive on pressure and a workload that others would find overwhelming. Not only must there be a large quantity of work, but it must also be interesting. Indeed, boredom is one of the primary reasons why top performers leave one employer for another. One of the ways to prevent boredom from setting in is to ask key employees for their views on the status of certain projects or how the department can run more efficiently. Also consider asking for their input when it comes to problem solving.

While top performers are largely responsible for making and aggressively pursuing their own opportunities, managers are also responsible for understanding top performers' goals and helping to clear a path leading to achievement. This means spending a good portion of the appraisal meeting discussing performance goals and career development.

Mentoring

Offering top performers mentoring opportunities may be just what's needed to keep this population motivated and challenged. Here's how it typically works:

"Mentoring" may be defined as a developmental, helping relationship whereby one person invests time, ability, and effort toward enhancing another person's growth, knowledge, and skills in preparation for greater productivity or future achievement. Mentoring relationships may be situational, informal, or formal. *Situational relationships* are short, isolated incidents involving a casual transfer of information or ideas from one person to another. *Informal mentoring* involves personal relationships in which one person voluntarily shares expertise or knowledge with another. *Formal mentoring programs* are more structured and focus on helping one or more individuals achieve specific goals.

Mentoring is a symbiotic relationship; that is, both mentors and mentees benefit. Mentees have the opportunity to achieve new performance objectives and further career development plans, and mentors are able to channel their skills and abilities in a new and personally rewarding direction.

Training mentors entails conveying what their role consists of, the amount of time and energy required, and the importance of confidentiality. Candidates for mentoring roles are selected on the basis of their skills, knowledge, availability, accessibility, interest, and rapport with potential mentees. Exactly how mentors and mentees communicate, and for how long, varies considerably, depending on the established objectives and learning styles of the mentees. Generally, mentoring programs last about a year.

• TIP #65 •

When it comes to evaluating top performers, your primary objective should be to keep them challenged.

Marginal Performers

No one will deny that it can be uncomfortable to tell employees that their work is anything less than outstanding. The task becomes all the more challenging when an employee's performance is marginal (read: poor; substandard; below average; subpar; unacceptable; fails to meet the requirements of the job; rarely meets the requirements of the job; never meets the requirements of the job; or fails to meet expectations).

Unfortunately, because it's hard to tell employees that their work is unacceptable, it's tempting to keep marginal performers around, avoiding what you perceive to be an inevitable confrontation. You may choose, instead, to tell these workers that their work is satisfactory, hoping that their performance will magically improve; that the employee will transfer or quit; or that you will be promoted and the employee will become someone else's headache.

Rarely does any of this actually happen, either because poor performers aren't motivated to change, or they don't know that aspects of their work are unacceptable. (Did someone say, "coaching and counseling"?)

Denial, then, isn't likely to work; nor is a tactless, all-out assault. Imagine bluntly informing an employee about her work, with no concern for her feelings, not to mention employment laws, employer-employee relations, or how HR is likely to respond. *Picture yourself as the manager in this scenario:* "Jean, what I'm about to say isn't personal; in fact, I like you: You're funny, and I admire the fact that you take in stray animals. But your work is really awful. You know this is true. You miss deadlines, don't follow instructions, and constantly use the wrong forms. I don't know why you don't just quit. It would make everyone in the department so happy, myself included. You'd probably be happier, too. Tell you what: Quit, and we'll meet once in a while for coffee."

Obviously, you could never, ever say anything even remotely similar to this. (I was uncomfortable just writing it.) But I'm willing to bet that you've had similar thoughts about an employee who won't leave on her own and whom no one has the nerve to terminate.

The fact of the matter is that dealing with a marginal performer doesn't necessitate resorting to one extreme or the other; that is, denial or verbal assassination. The key to successfully meeting with a marginal employee goes back to communicating about issues when they occur, thus making it far more likely that you will be able to summarize past performance during the appraisal meeting and move ahead to discuss methods for continued improvement and future goals.

Consider this scenario: Harry is a first-time manager in a small printing and graphics firm, promoted to his position just eight months ago. He's responsible for the work of three employees, two of whom he hired shortly after his promotion. Company policy dictates that all performance evaluations be conducted at the same time of year, and that date is rapidly approaching. Overall, he feels prepared, with one exception: He's uncomfortable about reviewing the work of an administrative assistant named Amy. He inherited Amy from his predecessor, Brent, who warned Harry about her surly attitude and spotty attendance. Brent had admittedly never spoken to Amy about her behavior, since he knew he was retiring soon and didn't want to bother. Now, it's up to Harry. In preparing for his meeting with Amy, Harry identifies the steps he believes will make meeting with Amy as palatable as possible:

- Talk with Brent concerning specific incidents during which Amy has demonstrated a "surly attitude."
- Talk with those with whom Amy has had regular contact to determine whether others view her as having a "surly attitude."
- Review Amy's attendance record to pinpoint what Brent has defined as "spotty."
- Obtain guidance from human resources.
- Remember to focus on the facts without personalizing the situation or succumbing to emotion.

This last point—focusing on facts without personalizing the situation—is Harry's key to succeeding with Amy. His ultimate goal is to help her perform to her maximum ability. This can only be accomplished if Amy is aware of how Harry views her work. That means being honest—something that is likely to generate any of a number of possible reactions from Amy

(Chapter 13). It also means supporting all of his statements with facts and making clear that the expectations he cites are job-related and not his, personally.

Brent failed Amy in this regard, and Harry needs to work twice as hard to accomplish his goal. Whether he succeeds is dependent on both Harry's determination and Amy's willingness to improve.

> ### • TIP #66 •
>
> It's hard to tell employees that their work is unacceptable. Instead, it's tempting to keep marginal performers around, hoping that the employee's performance will magically improve; that the employee will transfer or quit; or that you'll be promoted and the employee will become someone else's headache. Rarely does any of this actually happen.

•16•

Performance Appraisals for Employees Who Telecommute

Telecommuting is an alternative work arrangement whereby employees perform some percentage of their work at home or some other offsite location instead of regularly commuting to the office. Managers of employees who telecommute see these individuals on anywhere from a frequent to an occasional basis, and monitor their work through a combination of traditional and electronic means.

Employees who telecommute are generally expected to comply with the same policies and procedures as employees who commute to a traditional job site each day. This includes accomplishing clearly established tasks. As a manager, you are expected to appraise the performance of employees who telecommute just as you would with onsite employees.

• TIP #67 •

Telecommuting is an alternative work arrangement whereby employees perform some percentage of their work at home or some other offsite location instead of regularly commuting to the office.

Performance Monitoring

If you manage telecommuters, it's not unusual for you to express concern over the lack of direct control that you feel you have over their work. You have enough to deal with as you monitor the performance of employees with whom you interact on a daily basis; assessing the work of employees who aren't around all the time can understandably result in an increased level of discomfort.

Here are some of the most commonly asked questions posed by first-time managers about the performance of telecommuting employees:

- How can I determine whether there's a situation that calls for coaching?
- How can I counsel an employee about violating a work-related policy before it spirals out of control, when I'm not there to ensure compliance?
- How can I measure a telecommuter's performance against the duties and responsibilities identified in his job description when I can't regularly check on his work, first hand?
- How can I determine how well an employee is able to cope with pressure and effectively balance multiple projects simultaneously when I'm not around to see?
- Can I really get to know an employee with whom I infrequently interact?

These concerns are all valid; they are also manageable. Addressing them begins with effective communication.

Communication

The importance of consistent and purposeful communication cannot be overemphasized. You and your telecommuting employees need to find the right balance of keeping each other updated and informed, without becoming a communication burden. The expression "Out of sight, out of mind" holds a great deal of truth when it comes to telecommuters. You may get so caught up in your own tasks that you fail to give the necessary attention to the efforts of this group of employees. That's why it's so important to maintain a practice of ongoing communication; that is, staying in touch regularly, through a variety of means.

Telephone Communication

Encourage regular voice contact with telecommuters, ideally on a daily basis. E-mails are great, but they cannot convey tone of voice, inflection, pauses in speech, or emphasis (forget about using caps—THEY ALWAYS MAKE IT APPEAR THAT THE PERSON IS YELLING.) These calls can include a discussion of problems, status reports, areas of accomplishment, questions, suggestions, and any other topic deemed appropriate.

These are check-in and catch-up calls. Preferably, a certain time during each workday should be designated "talk time," when both you and the employee are likely to be available: this shouldn't turn into a game of telephone tag. Note the reference to phone calls during the workday: Talking with telecommuters is part of your job; as such, it should not spill over into nonworking hours for either party.

Electronic Communication

Unquestionably, if not for technology, telecommuting relationships would be strained, if not altogether doomed. Electronic communication in the form of e-mails and instant messaging (IMs), as well as web meetings, virtual bulletin boards, and videoconferencing, all facilitate virtual interactions, allowing for exchanges that are as close to "real" as you can get.

While it's true that electronic communication cannot substitute for face-to-face meetings or convey a person's tone of voice or vocal inflections, it does provide an instantaneous connection between you and telecommuting employees that can be enormously gratifying.

E-mails and IMs are clearly the electronic formats of choice.

Essentially, while the number of possible topics and content of e-mail messages are limitless, there are three basic e-mail communication categories:

• *Providing Information.* Here's an e-mail providing information, sent by a manager to one of her telecommuting employees working on a long-term project: "I'm including some additional resources you may find helpful in working on the Universal Synergy project. I've also attached a couple of related articles; hope you find that it provides interesting reading and some useful information."

• *Seeking Information.* This manager's e-mail could seek information by continuing with "Where did you put Universal's most recent status report?"

• *Requesting Action.* "Please send me a chronological list of everything you've discussed in meetings or otherwise covered with respect to Universal. I'll also need the corresponding spreadsheet. IM me today by 5 P.M. my time to verify. Thanks!"

In addition to providing and seeking information, and requesting action, e-mails enable you to share news from the home office; send photographs from company outings and parties; and mail e-cards with birthday greetings or messages of congratulations on a task.

• **TIP #68** •

The importance of consistent and purposeful communication cannot be overemphasized. This can be accomplished through regular voice contact and electronic communication in the form of e-mails, instant messaging, web meetings, virtual bulletin boards, and videoconferencing.

Face-to-Face Communication

As previously stated, no electronic communication tool or technique can substitute for the visual cues provided through body language or an auditory exchange between you and your workers. This includes web meetings and videoconferencing. Most telecommuters work within a reasonable geographic proximity to their managers, thus making periodic face-to-face meetings possible. What's considered a reasonable location? Truthfully, just about anywhere, although working at a site in Connecticut with a manager located in New York is going to be easier to negotiate than having an employee situated 3,000 miles away.

Logistics, then, will largely dictate the frequency of meetings. Most experts recommend, at a minimum, meeting with telecommuters one to four times per month, and more frequently when feasible. These meetings let employees know that the work they perform is important to the organization. It also reaffirms the employer-employee relationship and provides invaluable insight as to an individual's performance.

Avoid the trap of assuming that top or average performers require less personal attention than marginal employees (Chapter 15). Everyone requires strokes and constructive feedback. Try to time your meetings so that they coincide with celebratory events, such as the successful completion of a project or the opening of a new store. If you only commuticate when there are problems, employees will come to view you as the bearer of bad news.

• TIP #69 •

Most experts recommend meeting with telecommuters a minimum of one to four times per month, and more frequently when feasible.

Building a Relationship with Telecommuting Employees

Communicating regularly via telephone and e-mail and in person allows you to build relationships with your telecommuting employees. In a typical workplace setting, managers and workers get to know one another through numerous informal encounters: a casual conversation in the parking lot or elevator; a few words exchanged at the coffee machine or water cooler; or an impromptu visit by one to the other's office. In and of themselves, none of these occurrences is significant; however, together they serve to form the foundation that ultimately becomes a relationship between employer and employee. Through each encounter, over a period of days, weeks, and months, managers and employees learn a little bit more about one other.

Clearly, this "getting to know you" dance cannot be duplicated with telecommuting employees. It can, however, be modified and still have a positive impact. Consider the manager with a virtual water cooler. He invites his telecommuting employees to spend time with him at his cooler on a regular basis, just hanging out, talking about whatever happens to come up. While this is basically instant messaging, the fact that it's called a "water cooler" and emphasizes nonwork topics makes it more manager-friendly. In essence, the manager is building a virtual workplace community that encourages everyone to get to know one another better, just as they might if they were working in the same office every day.

Building a relationship with telecommuting employees is also more likely to occur if you stress the degree of trust that you have in their ability to do their jobs in a timely fashion. This can be challenging, as you might understandably feel uneasy about your lack of control over the work being performed offsite. You can't physically see them doing their jobs, overhear phone conversations, ensure a full day's work, or even know whether they're where they're supposed to be. (Consider the employee who was "busted" because he was seen at the beach when he was supposed to be at home, working.)

If you feel stressed over not being able to monitor employee performance personally, consider the words of advice offered by the memorable character Loretta Castorini, in *Moonstruck*: "Snap out of it!" You shouldn't be hovering over employees in the office, and the fact that you can't hover over telecommuting employees just means that you're managing the way you should anyway. Assign a task, and leave the person alone to do his job. Be available for help (on- or off-site), but otherwise step aside. Don't you have enough of your own work to do?

Successful telecommuting relationships are predicated on managers having sufficient confidence in their own ability to manage, and trust in the employees they have working for them—whether in the office or offsite. It's a simple fact: when employees feel that they are trusted, they are more likely to contribute at a high level. Reassure employees that you have confidence in their ability to perform their jobs and then let them demonstrate what they can do.

Performance Measurement

If you manage on-site employees, chances are you're process-focused. Notably, you measure and assess the effectiveness of a worker's performance based, in part, on the degree of effort expended, offering positive and corrective feedback in the form of coaching and counseling, as warranted. When it comes to telecommuting employees, however, you may find it difficult to advise, assess, and give feedback to workers who aren't physically there. As such, you need to shift your focus to results; that is, judge employees on output, not "face time." Stated another way, concentrate on measuring productivity, not activity. Your commitment should be to evaluate employees based on how well mutually agreed-upon goals are achieved, rather than on what you observe on a daily basis.

Measurement Criteria

Earlier in this chapter, you read some of the most commonly asked questions posed by managers about the performance of remote employees. Let's revisit these questions and see what measurement criteria pertain:

Q: *How can I determine whether there's a situation that calls for coaching?*

A: Managing off-site employees warrants an expansion of the 360-degree evaluation. Rather than relying on feedback from individuals with whom the telecommuting employee has contact solely at the time of the formal appraisal, regularly communicate with them to identify areas that might call for assistance, support, praise, and constructive criticism. You can also periodically solicit self-appraisals. In addition, daily telephone conversations and frequent e-mails are likely to reveal situations that call for coaching.

Q: *How can I counsel an employee about violating a work-related policy before it spirals out of control, when I'm not there to ensure compliance?*

A: If feedback from individuals with whom the telecommuting employee has contact reveals performance concerns, you must address them immediately. This should be accomplished face-to-face, with you going to the employee's work site, not the other way around. As with coaching, the essence of counseling is the same with telecommuters as it is for on-site employees; that is, following a sequence of steps, the goal of which is to rectify a work-related issue.

Q: *How can I measure a telecommuting employee's performance against the duties and responsibilities identified in his job description when I can't check on his work, first hand?*

A: Provide telecommuters with copies of their job descriptions. At least quarterly, ask them to review the content and submit a report to you, identifying specific areas where they feel they excel and/or need improvement. Require supporting examples. In addition, if feasible, pose the question: "If I were to ask [name of someone familiar with the position] to measure your performance against the duties and responsibilities identified in your job description, what would she say?

Q: *How can I determine how well an employee is able to cope with pressure and effectively balance multiple projects simultaneously when I'm not around to see?*

A: For each project, create a task list; then check off items as they are completed. Depending on the complexity of these tasks, you can request progress reports at regular intervals, identifying the following: overall and specific objectives; steps; timelines; individual components; resources available;

resources used; projected time required for completion; and actual time required for completion.

Q: *Can I really get to know an employee with whom I infrequently interact?*

A: Yes. Communicate often and through varied means, including daily telephone calls, frequent e-mails, and regularly scheduled face-to-face meetings. Be patient; getting to know anyone takes time. Learning about a telecommuting employee is not so different from becoming acquainted with the behaviors and work habits of an onsite worker.

• TIP #70 •

If you manage telecommuting employees, concentrate on measuring productivity, not activity.

Appendix A: List of Performance-Appraisal Tips

Tip #1: The primary objective of a performance appraisal is to ensure the maximum utilization of every employee's skills, knowledge, and interests.

Tip #2: Secondary performance-appraisal objectives include enhancing employer-employee relations; permitting HR to perform key tasks more effectively; and motivating employees to pursue goals that are compatible with organizational goals.

Tip#3: The most effective performance-appraisal programs are those that are beneficial to managers, employees, and the organization as a whole.

Tip #4: While HR has the greatest scope of responsibility when it comes to performance appraisals, managers and employees should also actively participate in the process.

Tip #5: In order for a performance-appraisal system to function effectively, it must be: job-related; reliable and valid; standardized; practical and workable; acceptable to everyone in the organization; reflective of a managerial style that is conducive to employee growth; and predicated on a managerial willingness to offer suggestions for improved performance.

Tip #6: Coaching is the day-to-day interaction between you and your employees. Its purpose is to provide regular assistance, support, praise, and constructive criticism.

Tip #7: To be an effective coach, you should strive to be approachable, consistent, dependable, empathetic, honest, knowledgeable, and respectful.

Tip #8: Spontaneous coaching requires you to be attentive and attuned to each employee's individual work habits, routines, and current assignments. This principle pertains to both positive and negative performance.

Tip #9: Planned coaching allows you to seek out an opportune time to focus on a situation, but it is still informal in terms of the approach.

Tip #10: Counseling is the structured interaction between managers and their employees, with a keener focus on specific work-related problems.

Tip #11: To be effective in your role as a counselor, strive to be attentive, broad-minded, committed, conscientious, focused, interested, and realistic.

Tip #12: The directive-counseling approach requires you to identify the problem, tell the employee why it's a problem, and then tell the employee what he or she needs to do to rectify the matter. This approach rarely achieves the desired outcome.

Tip #13: The nondirective-counseling approach calls for a partnership between you and your employees, with each having a specified role. Because the employee has greater control over her own behavior, the nondirective approach is more likely to result in positive change.

Tip #14: Ongoing coaching and counseling set the stage for the performance-review meeting; that is, by doing your job as an effective coach and counselor, you will be prepared to apply successfully the three golden rules of performance appraisal.

Tip #15: *Golden Rule #1:* Nothing that is said during a performance appraisal should ever come as a surprise to an employee.

Tip #16: *Golden Rule #2:* Always strive to include both praise and constructive criticism when conducting performance appraisals.

Tip #17: *Golden Rule #3:* Document every incident that is referenced in a performance appraisal.

Tip #18: An important aspect of getting ready for the appraisal meeting is gathering and comparing information from several sources.

Tip #19: Before conducting appraisals, review those qualifications that are necessary to do a job, and clearly identify the specific tasks that employees are expected to perform. This is best accomplished in the form of a job description.

Tip #20: With the 360-degree method of appraisal, performance input is received from the manager as well as several additional sources. This is done to provide a well-rounded evaluation and to enhance employee development and growth.

Tip #21: Self-evaluations allow employees to compare their own assessments with those of their managers, and vice versa.

Tip #22: A lot can change when a former coworker becomes a manager, impacting every aspect of the relationship. Before reviewing the work of former colleagues, you should clarify respective roles and establish expectations.

Tip #23: Clarification of new respective roles and responsibilities between you and former coworkers affects all aspects of performance appraisals, including coaching and counseling.

Tip #24: While your promotion might not impact the actual duties and responsibilities of your former coworkers, the change in your working relationship can alter their performance. Therefore, it's important to learn what your former coworkers expect of you as their manager, as well as to make known your expectations of them.

Tip #25: Addressing issues and not personalities, focusing on work-related matters, and treating former coworkers the same as other employees can help you remain focused as you prepare to conduct appraisals on former coworkers.

Tip #26: The ideal performance-appraisal form combines descriptive terms requiring supporting comments with providing ample space for employees to comment on their manager's evaluation.

Tip #27: Performance-appraisal forms are maximally effective when they are used to highlight an employee's performance from the last review, or date of hire, to the present, in relation to the requirements and responsibilities as identified in the job description.

Tip #28: The most effective way to avoid problems associated with five-, four-, or three-term ratings is to require supporting statements and examples to accompany each rating.

Tip #29: The factors appearing on a performance-appraisal form are usually generic in nature. As such, they should be defined in clear and concise terms so that everyone interprets them the same way.

Tip #30: Language selected for written performance appraisals should be objective. Objective language is impartial and likely to be interpreted similarly by most people. Conversely, subjective language reflects one's personal opinion, may be subject to interpretation, and fails to communicate relevant, concrete information.

Tip #31: Conveying a certain written tone and using a particular writing style will set the stage for a maximally productive face-to-face meeting. Simply stated, your tone should be direct, factual, and positive; your style moderate to formal, with limited jargon and clichés.

Tip #32: The success of any performance-appraisal program is rooted in consistency and uniformity; that is, all mangers following the same format so employees know they are being evaluated according to the same standards as everyone else.

Tip #33: Following a seven-step format for written reviews ensures consistency and uniformity. The format consists of: providing an overview; identifying employee strengths; identifying areas requiring improvement; reviewing success in meeting previously agreed-upon goals; setting new goals; identifying career-development plans; and soliciting employee feedback.

Tip #34: What takes place at the beginning of a performance appraisal meeting sets the tone for the rest of the meeting.

Tip #35: Ask yourself some key questions just prior to conducting face-to-face performance-appraisal meetings to maximally ensure that employees receive fair and objective evaluations.

Tip #36: There are four essential ingredients to creating a suitable environment: privacy, a distraction-free location, comfort, and adequate time.

Tip #37: Regardless of how well you know your employees, be sure to devote time at the beginning of the meeting to ensure that they feel at ease.

Tip #38: The most successful performance-appraisal meetings are those that focus on three distinct areas: past performance; previous and future performance objectives; and the employee's career-development plan.

Tip #39: The portion of the meeting devoted to past performance may best be viewed as a summary, laying the foundation for the rest of the meeting.

Tip #40: If you've done your job throughout the year as a coach and counselor, employees will know in advance of the appraisal meeting how successful they've been in meeting previously set goals.

Tip #41: During the future goal-setting stage of an appraisal meeting, you can ask questions and make suggestions, but the employee needs to do the bulk of the planning and work.

Tip #42: Successful goal setting hinges on clearly stating the performance objective; breaking the objective down into identifiable and manageable components; isolating resources needed to accomplish each component; identifying possible barriers; and developing a timeline.

Tip #43: Helping an employee develop a career plan involves three steps: a discussion of the employee's career objectives; consideration of additional education, training, or experience needed; and implementation in relation to the employee's current job.

Tip #44: Active listening entails absorbing the meaning, intent, and purpose behind a person's words.

Tip #45: To maximize your ability to listen actively, concentrate on themes, not words; summarize periodically to ensure a clear picture of what the employee is telling you; filter out distractions; screen out personal biases; and acknowledge any unusual emotional states that could influence your ability to concentrate.

Tip #46: During the performance-appraisal meeting, try to allocate no more than 25 pecent of the time to talking, devoting the remainder of time to active listening.

Tip #47: Instead of viewing silence as a negative, you can use it to bolster your active listening skills by seeing silence as a means to an end; that is, an opportunity to learn more about an employee's thoughts concerning his past performance, goals, or career-development plans.

Tip #48: Verbal messages are considered less persuasive than nonverbal ones; hence, when there is a discrepancy between the verbal and the nonverbal, the nonverbal is often more influential.

Tip #49: We often respond to false assumptions by quickly assigning specific meaning to gestures, movements, and expressions.

Tip #50: Alone, positive gestures and movements can send a strong message; combined, the potential impact is even greater.

Tip #51: You are responsible for conveying unambiguous nonverbal communication.

Tip #52: Accurately assess nonverbal messages conveyed by an employee by identifying individual patterns over time.

Tip #53: Illustrators do not have a specific meaning that can be pinpointed; rather, they serve to support a person's words, providing consistency between nonverbal and verbal messages.

Tip #54: Coaching and counseling throughout the evaluation period should enable you to develop a fairly solid sense of how employees are likely to respond to an appraisal. Still, unexpected responses can occur.

Tip #55: There are six employee behavior patterns that employees typically exhibit during performance-appraisal meetings: agreement; argument; defensiveness; nervousness; overconfidence; and silence.

Tip #56: Performance-appraisal meetings with employees who exhibit unexpected traits can become productive encounters.

Tip #57: Developing a keener understanding of employee goals is one possible outcome of accommodating differing responses to a performance appraisal.

Tip #58: Performance appraisals may lay the foundation for, and thus lead to, disciplinary action, including termination, despite your best efforts to help an employee improve performance or behavior.

Tip #59: The law is clear when it comes to using discriminatory language in the performance-appraisal process: Don't do it. You can avoid being accused of using discriminatory language by focusing on job-related facts, rather than personal characteristics.

Tip #60: Avoid committing to something that might happen in the future. This is called an "implied contract" and could result in charges of discrimination if what you promised doesn't materialize.

Tip #61: Despite all your efforts and best intentions, it's still possible to fall into typical performance-appraisal pitfalls and to be influenced by factors to the extent that they become counterproductive patterns of behavior. When applied to conducting performance appraisals, these patterns may be categorized as specific types of syndromes.

Tip #62: Avoid trying to commit to memory all that should be covered during a performance-appraisal session. Instead, keep a checklist nearby, identifying key areas.

Tip #63: All employees, regardless of their level of performance, need feedback.

Tip #64: Average performers are the largest population of most organizations. As such, by virtue of sheer numbers, they form the foundation of any business and should not be ignored when it comes to performance appraisals.

Tip #65: When it comes to evaluating top performers, your primary objective should be to keep them challenged.

Tip #66: It's hard to tell employees that their work is unacceptable. Instead, it's tempting to keep marginal performers around, hoping that the employee's performance will magically improve; that the employee will transfer or quit; or that you'll be promoted and the employee will become someone else's headache. Rarely does any of this actually happen.

Tip #67: Telecommuting is an alternative work arrangement whereby employees perform some percentage of their work at home or some other offsite location instead of regularly commuting to the office.

Tip #68: The importance of consistent and purposeful communication cannot be overemphasized. This can be accomplished through regular voice contact and electronic communication in the form of e-mails, instant messaging, web meetings, virtual bulletin boards, and videoconferencing.

Tip #69: Most experts recommend meeting with telecommuters a minimum of one to four times per month, and more frequently when feasible.

Tip #70: If you manage telecommuting employees, concentrate on measuring productivity, not activity.

Appendix B:
Key Federal Legislation

The Civil Rights Act of 1964 prohibits discrimination on the basis of race, color, religion, sex, and national origin in all matters of employment.

The Equal Pay Act of 1963 requires equal pay for men and women performing substantially equal work.

The Age Discrimination in Employment Act of 1967 prohibits discrimination in all matters of employment, regardless of how old the employee is.

The Americans with Disabilities Act of 1990 prohibits discrimination against individuals with disabilities.

The Pregnancy Discrimination Act of 1978 states that women who are pregnant must be permitted to work as long as they are capable of performing the essential functions of their current job or any job to which they have been promoted or transferred.

The Immigration Reform and Control Act of 1986 prohibits discrimination against individuals on the basis of citizenship or national origin in all matters of employment.

The Civil Rights Act of 1991 extends coverage afforded by the Civil Rights Act of 1964 by providing additional remedies for intentional discrimination and unlawful harassment in the workplace.

Copies of these laws may be obtained from:

Equal Employment Opportunity Commission (EEOC)
U.S. Department of Labor
1801 L Street NW
Washington, D.C. 20507
Phone: 202-663-4900
http://www.eeoc.gov/

Index